MEDIA MANUALS

Creating Special Effects
for TV and Films

MEDIA MANUALS

Creating
Special
Effects
for TV
and Film

Bernard
Wilkie

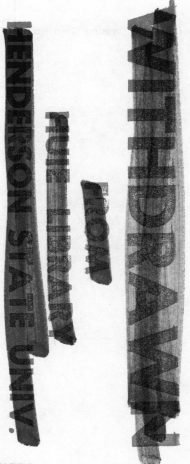
A Focal Press Book

Communication Arts Books
HASTINGS HOUSE, PUBLISHERS
New York, NY 10016

ISBN 8038-1209-4
Library of Congress Catalog Card No: 77-77829

Printed and Bound in England by A. Wheaton & Co., Exeter.

Contents

Introduction

The purpose of this book is to give a simple, basic guide to the design and use of special effects and props in film and television production. Diagrams and illustrations supplement the text and where applicable materials and methods of manufacture are also explained. The subjects and techniques outlined have been carefully selected to give a comprehensive range of principles. It will be seen that these principles can be permuted in many ways, giving a variety of solutions to a variety of problems.

For visual effects to appear convincing as much depends on the way in which they are used as on their original design. Notes for directors have therefore been included in some of the subjects.

Acknowledgement
The author would like to thank the Head of Television Design of the British Broadcasting Corporation for permission to publish this book.

Some Useful Tools

To create his props and devices the effects designer uses hand and machine tools ranging across many trades and crafts. There are, however, certain aids which assist him in producing his effects in the studio and without which the final results might be disappointing.

Viewfinder

All film and television pictures take place within a specific frame and therefore a good zoom viewfinder is a very useful adjunct to composition. With it the effects designer can frame his shots both in the studio and when shooting model sequences. Many items of effects apparatus have to be situated on the edge of the scene and accurate framing can prevent wasted space or unwanted intrusions into the picture. Used for model shots the viewfinder helps to determine the most suitable camera viewpoint and is also useful for establishing the perspective.

Monochrome glass

The monochromatic glass (or pan-glass) is useful for studying scenes in colour where the eventual recorded or transmitted picture is to be in black and white. The glass, a near monochromatic 'yellow', gives an approximation of the tones that will appear in the final picture.

Colour chart

The colour chart shows the monochromatic equivalent of the main range of colours. It is necessary to study this chart when designing props and models for use in television where the service is transmitting in both colour and black and white. What may look good in colour can sometimes present the black-and-white viewer with a series of uniformly grey tones, lacking contrast and form.

Small-format movie camera

An 8mm movie camera is useful when it is required to test effects beforehand. It allows results to be studied carefully both at normal speed and frame by frame. Furthermore the fact that the resultant film can be screened anywhere means that viewing is not limited to the time that can be booked in a special screening room or rushes theatre.

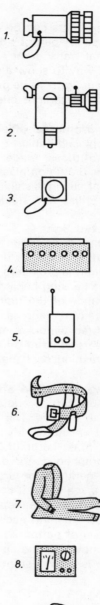

People who are employed to provide special effects for films and television have to make use of – and rely upon – many tools and items of a specialised nature. These may be needed at short notice and as the work for which they are required is often hazardous it is essential that they are kept in first class condition. It is advisable therefore that the items shown here in colour become the personal responsibility of those who are going to use them. 1, Zoom viewfinder. 2, 8mm cine camera. 3, Pan glass. 4, Firing box. 5, Radio-control unit. 6, Safety harness and ropes. 7, Wet suit and diving gear. 8. Test meter and firing circuit meter. 9. Personal tool kit.

Light and shade create convincing illusions.

Projected Light Effects

Certain effects can be achieved by using light either in the form of a projected image or by bouncing the light off a reflective surface. A conventional transparency or slide, for example, can be projected in the normal way to show a still picture. The second method allows moving shapes or lights to be projected. Typical of this is the mirror-ball used to create the starlight effect in ballrooms.

Static projected effects
Masks placed behind the lens of a slide projector can cast shadows to simulate those made by scenic items. Black lines in rectangular patterns drawn on glass plates can be beamed on to the set to give the effect of sunlight shining through bars of a window. Open doorways, prison grilles and stained-glass windows are other examples.

Reflected light
The flame-drum (page 74) may be used to create moving train effects. Undulating lines are drawn in matt paint around the shiny drum and white light is projected on to its rotating surface. The reflections picked up on a backing behind the windows of an underground train give the appearance of the tunnel rushing past.

A line of rectangular mirrors fastened to the drum gives the effect of the lighted windows of a train passing through a station at night. ·

Smears of paint on the drum can be made to look like fast-moving cloud rushing past the windows of an aircraft.

Moving projected effects
Projectors can be equipped with revolving transparent slides to create recurring images. The slides, usually in the form of glass discs, are rotated on motor driven spindles.

The most common is the cloudscape with the clouds painted or photographed on the disc in a continuous circle. The projected picture moves gently in an arc, but this is seldom considered objectionable.

For a sea effect it is possible to paint or photograph a horizontal ripple effect on three rectangular glass sheets which are slowly moved up and down behind each other.

Pieces of patterned glass can be used to create interesting effects when moved in the light of a projector, but the quality and size of the picture is often determined by the amount of illumination available.

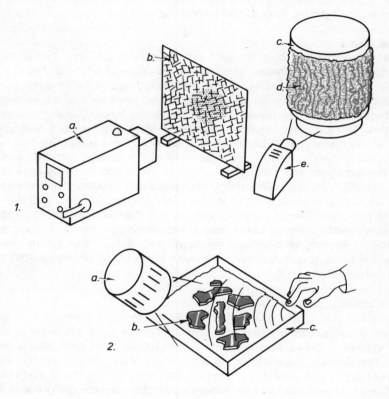

PROJECTED LIGHT EFFECTS

1. Backings for performers

Projected in this way, light can be used to provide large superimposed backings for performers appearing in front of a second camera.

a, TV camera. b, Sheet of patterned glass. c, Revolving drum. d, Screwed-up aluminium foil. e, Projector light.

2. Water ripples

This set-up produces the water ripple effect associated with sea and shipboard scenes.

a, Lamp. b, Pieces of broken mirror. c, Tray of water.

Mattes and Glass Shots

There are many ways of increasing the area of a scene without building scenery or adding to the amount of floor space. The techniques used not only give additional dimensions, but also permit effects to be obtained that might be impossible in real terms.

Matte shots

These are usually associated with film, the TV equivalent being the electronic inlay and overlay devices for obtaining similar results.

Briefly, a film matte is the process by which part of a frame is left unexposed so that it can later be used to record another picture. In this way two components may be used to produce a single picture on one negative. The simplest example is where a black card is positioned in front of the camera so that only half a picture is recorded. The film is then rewound without moving the position of the camera and the black card is repositioned to obscure the part of the scene that has already been filmed. The composite picture is called a split screen. It permits an actor to appear as two people in the same shot.

Matte work is the province of the cameraman and the processing laboratories and involves some very complicated processes. The most versatile is known as travelling matte where backgrounds can be inserted behind actors who have previously played their scene against a coloured backing.

Glass shots

Glass shots are often used where it is required to show a ceiling without actually constructing one. The technique is to set a sheet of glass in front of the camera and for the false ceiling to be painted directly on the glass. This must be done with constant reference to the camera eyepiece to ensure that the painting lines up with the studio set. The size of the painting and its distance from the camera are governed by the fact that both scene and foreground glass must be in focus.

As the sheet of glass reflects anything in front of it, the camera must be in a darkened area or surrounded by black drapes.

Glass is used when particularly fine work or disconnected items have to appear in the scene, but there are many instances when it can be dispensed with and a simple cardboard cut-out employed. This is possible when skies, landscapes or seascapes are included in a scene.

The card, painted to blend with the scenery, can be made to match at some convenient natural boundary – such as the horizon or the ridge of a roof. For a false ceiling for studio scenes the tops of flats on the set and the bottom of a piece of card blend quite satisfactorily.

The glass shot does not always require the work of an artist: cut-out photographs, provided they are big enough, can be used to supplement the scene.

14

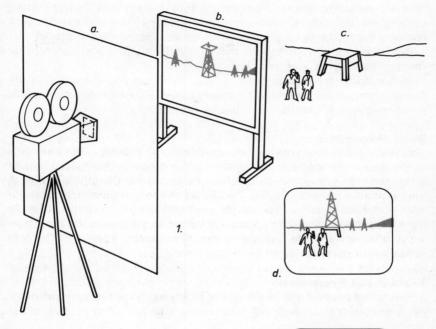

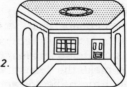

MATTES AND GLASS SHOTS

1. Painted scenery

By using pictures painted on glass much time and money can be saved in construction of scenery. The example shown here demonstrates how the top half of an oil rig is aligned with a scenic base built on location. Reflections in the glass can be troublesome and black boards – or even complete black cabins – must be erected to shield the glass. a, Black sheet, b, Painted glass. c, Scenic base. d. Final picture.

2. Ceilings

The painted glass technique is often used to provide ceilings for interior sets in the studio.

Scenic Projection

This is the system where large photographic backgrounds are projected on a screen behind the action. It is cheap, easy to use and enables very realistic indoor or outdoor scenes to be re-created in the studio.

It can be employed in both movie and TV studios and can provide moving as well as static backgrounds.

When moving subjects are required, the recording camera and the projector must be interlocked to ensure that the shutter of the camera is synchronised with the shutter of the projector.

Back Projection
This is the oldest and most widely used form of projection, but demands more studio space than other systems. The projector is situated behind a transluscent screen which itself is placed behind the studio scene. A very powerful projector is required because the screen absorbs a great deal of the illumination. To obtain maximum benefit from the available light the camera should be positioned on the same axis as the projector.

Smaller set-ups are used to obtain the moving scenes in the rear windows of cars in the studio.

Front Axial Projection
This is more economical in the use of space as the projector is positioned in front of the screen which can therefore be placed at the rear of the studio.

The screen, consisting of a flexible material covered with millions of tiny glass beads has the unique property of being able to reflect the light that strikes it back along the path from which it came.

This of course implies that all the light is reflected back to the projector. To make the system work it is necessary to install a beam-splitter between the projector and the recording camera so that some of the light returning from the screen is diverted to the camera. The screen material reflects so efficiently that a domestic 35mm slide projector can be used to provide large background scenes, while light reflected from actors in the projector beam is insufficient to affect the film.

Application
Front-axial screen material can be cut up and used to provide multi-plane layouts. For instance a projected picture of a house against sky could be split into two parts, the house being beamed on to a profiled cut-out and the sky on to the studio backing. A person walking from behind the cut-out would appear to come from behind the house. Useful for Lilliputian scenes where small people walk around large objects.

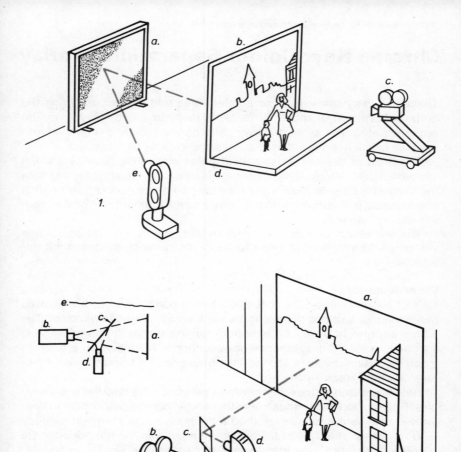

SCENIC PROJECTION

1. Back projection
Easy to set up and use, back projection requires a lot of studio space. Large mirrors are used to reduce the distance from projector to screen.
a, Mirror. b, Translucent screen. c, Camera. d, Stage. e, Movie projector.

2. Front axial projection
More care is needed in setting up, but front axial projection uses no extra studio space and provides brighter pictures. It also permits the background picture to be split up into layers if profiled pieces of reflex screen material are positioned in front of the action.
a, Reflex screen. b, Camera. c, Semi-transparent mirror. d, Projector. e, Black backing. f, Free standing profiled screen faced with reflex material.

17

Chroma Key: Colour Separation Overlay

These are the names given to an electronic method of combining the outputs from two or more TV cameras or other sources (such as film scanners, etc.). The system allows parts of one picture to be inlaid into another in such a way that the divisions cannot be detected.

The brain of the device is an electronic switch that 'flips' over when fed with a certain colour signal from the primary picture. If for instance the control colour is blue, wherever that blue appears in the original scene the switch automatically removes it and substitutes pictures from the second source.

The equipment is highly selective so that only the precise colour hue will trigger the switch, all other tones of the same colour leaving it un-affected.

What it can do

One of its chief assets is that it enables backgrounds to be inserted behind actors without the necessity for a scenic projection system. The actors perform in front of a blue backing and the background scene is supplied either from a transparency scanner or from film on a telecine machine. Alternatively, a second TV camera can be framed up on a picture or photograph in the studio.

Actors dressed in blue performing against a blue backing are invisible. This is useful for those effects where disembodied heads float around or where a person, clothed fully in blue, can manipulate props without being seen. Similarly a flying-carpet can be supported on a framework painted blue and appear to float in the sky.

The chroma key/CSO equipment is often used for caption effects. Letters on coloured backgrounds can be combined with moving film or studio shots to give any variety of effects.

Free-standing cut-outs painted blue can be used to divide the inserted material into layers. This permits actors to work around various components of the inlaid scene. For example, the crates and boxes in a warehouse scene might be no more than sections of profiled plywood coloured blue.

Limitations

Actors placed in front of blue-painted backings are bound to be illuminated from behind with that colour. This leads to coloured fringing which shows against the inserted background. Yellow is sometimes less disturbing than blue for that reason.

Any shiny surface will reflect the colour of the backing, causing break-up of the signal in that area.

Inserted backgrounds remain constant so any movement of the camera taking the primary scene cannot be tolerated.

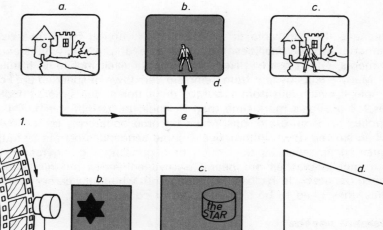

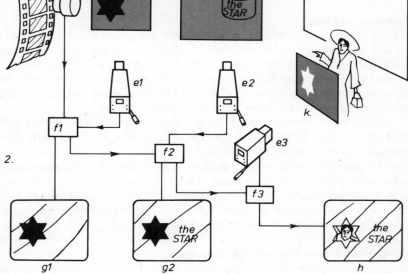

CHROMA KEY/COLOUR SEPARATION OVERLAY

1. Switching colour

The control colour switches the output from one camera to another.

a, Output from camera 1. b, Output from camera 2. c, Transmitted picture. d, Switching colour. e, Switching unit.

2. Chroma key operation

A number of sources can be combined in one final picture. This is useful for caption effects, but also has application in scenic effects.

a, Telecine film scanner. b, Caption. c, Moving caption in front of backing. d, Performer in front of backing. e, T.V. Cameras. f, Switch units. g, Outputs. h, Transmitted picture. k, Cut-out.

Film Cameras

Because they are able to expose film at varying frame speeds film cameras provide facilities not obtainable at present with electronic cameras, which need a fixed time to scan each individual frame.

Many effects benefit from being slowed down or speeded up. For example, if a man falls from a roof top the action appears more effective if his fall occupies more time than it would at normal speed. This also applies to some explosions which become apparently more powerful when slowed down. Alternatively, some sequences benefit from being speeded up, such as the action of a gunslinger going for his Colt. Automobile crashes are nearly always enhanced by this technique when the action is in close up. In long-shot when they career over cliff--tops, they need to be slowed down of course.

Camera speeds

A high filming speed is used to slow down the action when projected. A slow filming speed is used to speed things up. There are, of course, limits to the speeds, both slow and fast, to which cameras can be run. Where very high speeds are required, special equipment must be obtained. Nevertheless most 16mm and 35mm cameras are capable of being run at speeds slower and faster than normal.

High speed cameras use a lot of film. Many dozens of feet pass through the gate as the camera motor gets up to speed and many more are wasted as it slows down again.

One problem encountered with high speed filming is the necessity to provide sufficient light. The faster the speed the more light is required and this often implies that the lights have to be positioned very close to the subject. In the case of model shots this can mean that the materials of the model are subjected to intense local heating.

Stop-frame and time-lapse cameras

Single-frame cameras used for cartoon and animation work are invariably custom-built for their particular purposes. Ordinary cameras designed for normal running may not hold each frame sufficiently steady to prevent the completed film from showing obvious signs of 'hunting'.

Stop frame cameras are usually operated remotely by solenoid and cable to avoid camera movement. Exposures with time-lapse cameras are invariably controlled by a time switch set to operate the shutter at pre-determined intervals. The timing device is also used to switch on the lights prior to a take and to switch them off afterwards. It is important to allow sufficient time for the lamps to warm up if the resultant film is to be flicker-free.

Explosions
Model shots featuring explosions require to be filmed at high speed to slow the action down.

Falls
Dramatic sequences such as men falling from buildings often benefit from prolonged motion. These call for the high speed camera.

Car chase
A car chase in which the driver must negotiate tricky or hazardous obstacles looks more impressive if the action is speeded up. This requires a slow speed camera.

Fights
Fight sequences are enhanced if the speed of action is increased. This calls for a slowed-down camera.

21

Animation Stand Camerawork

Although animation is not generally considered to be the province of the effects designer, there are occasions when filmed animation can produce results that would be difficult to achieve by other means.

Animation is carried out by photographing drawings, cels, photographs etc. – and sometimes even three-dimensional objects – on a stand above which is mounted a camera. The camera, capable of taking single frames or slow speed automatic runs is mounted on a shakeproof, vertical column. It can be moved up and down, the focus being automatically adjusted as it travels, giving a range of frame areas from close-up to long-shot. The bench is provided with controls which can be used to move the subject from side to side, up and down and also rotate it.

Generally photos, cels or drawings are produced on standard format material which has punched holes along one edge. These holes allow the illustrations to be accurately located on a peg bar.

Uses

To show the castle being covered in weeds and creepers for the story of *The Sleeping Beauty,* the hundred-year metamorphosis can be indicated by a series of slow dissolves with the growth of weeds increasing with each step. An artist's picture of the castle can be covered with a series of transparent cels on each of which the artist has drawn a further growth of vegetation.

A science programme showing stresses of bridges can use filmed photographs of existing bridges which have been cut and moved to show the bending movement that takes place under excessive loads.

A comedy programme showing a house falling down can also make use of a photograph. Pre-cut, and with each piece moved a fraction of an inch for each successive frame of film, the house finishes up as a bizarre heap at the bottom of the frame.

Preparation

Before undertaking any animation it is usual to draw up a storyboard of the action. This defines not only the action but also the time scale. At 24 frames of film a second, it is a simple matter to calculate what distance any component must travel in a given time. The time is assessed with a stop watch while miming the action on a sheet of paper.

When many separate components are being moved it is advisable to prepare a chart and tick off each item once it has been moved. Without this it is very easy to forget whether a piece has been moved or not.

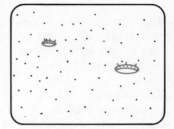

Techniques
Animation stand techniques are particularly useful for creating moving starscapes, 'travelling-through-space' shots etc.

Filming photographs
The animation stand camera is used to film photographs of models to create space sequences.

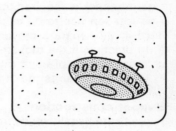

Animated graphics
Superimposed electronically or projected on to a screen, animated graphics filmed on the animation stand may be used for demonstration purposes.

Combination shots
Pictures filmed and animated on the animation stand may later be combined with filmed action shot normally. This mix is carried out by optical printing.

Stop-Frame Film Animation

This is the technique used in the making of puppet films and commercials where inanimate objects appear to move. The items being filmed are moved a fraction at a time, each movement being recorded on a single frame of film.

Technique

Before commencing filming, it is advisable to make a chart of the movements required. Normal film projection is at 24 frames a second and all movement is consequently related to this yardstick.

Each movement is first assessed in real time. Say, for example, that a cigarette pack is required to spin at the rate of one revolution a second. This rotation has to be calculated on the basis that the pack revolves once in 24 separate movements.

In practice, if the movement is too small, it is possible to shoot two or more frames of each position.

Slow movements look realistic, but fast ones often appear jerky.

Puppet construction

Puppets are usually made from flexible material modelled on aluminium wire armatures. They should be 'dead' with no trace of springiness. During animation it should be possible to pin their feet to the baseboard so that one limb is always firmly located. Hours of patient filming can be ruined if a puppet shifts accidently during animation.

Points to remember

Used on the set, stop-frame animation is a painstaking and laborious process and when complicated sequences are envisaged it is sensible to plan the operation with this in mind. If all the furniture in a room is to dance around, the operational fatigue of walking into the set, moving a cupboard a fraction of an inch, and then a chair, and then the bed etc., before shooting just one single frame should be carefully considered beforehand.

Before each exposure the cameraman must check the scene to ensure that the operators' shadows are not in the frame.

Another thing likely to ruin the whole sequence is the accidental displacement of any object. Never situate awkward items in the paths of the operators who might have to go to and fro many hundreds of times. Similarly, when small table-top objects are being manipulated it is easy to catch some static component with the hand or sleeve. All items not required to be animated should be firmly fixed.

When filming outdoors, care must be taken that the operators do not tread on the grass or loose surfaces within the frame. Grass that has been walked upon fluctuates madly in the finished print.

Eccentric movement

Exposing a frame at a time, a golf ball can be filmed performing strange antics around the green.

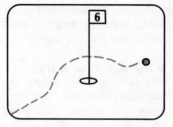

Animated commercials

Commercials rely a great deal on the versatility of the stop-frame camera.

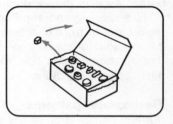

Unbelievable action

Fantasy can be filmed using stop-motion techniques. The scene pictured here would switch from the cyclist as he neared the wall to a dummy (replacing him on the bicycle) being pulled into the air.

Captions and titles

Stop motion techniques are frequently used to achieve unusual effects for captions and title sequences.

THE SONG Special...

Live Animated Diagrams

It is possible to screen quite interesting animated pictures and diagrams using simple paper cut-outs manipulated by hand. These animated pictures are usually constructed from card, paper and balsa wood.

Simple movements

The simplest movement of all is the removal of a piece of paper covering something that has to appear on cue. An example might be a bottle drawn in outline. The inside of the bottle is cut out and a similarly coloured piece of card placed behind. A strip of differently coloured paper inserted between the two cards appears as the contents of the bottle. As it is drawn downward, the bottle appears to empty.

To show a graph apparently drawing itself, the line is first drawn on plain card. In front of this is placed another card with a cut out rectangular void. Horizontal and vertical datum lines are added by fastening thin elastic cords to the front card. A sheet of similarly coloured card need only to be pulled out sideways for the line to produce itself.

Flashes and patterns

If areas or cut-outs on the diagram are required to flash it is a simple matter to pass alternating light and dark colours behind them. This can be achieved by painting the appropriate patterns on revolving discs or sliding strips of paper. Cut-out slots radiating star fashion from a single point can have behind them a disc on which has been painted a similar number of lines. Revolving the disc produces a flashing sequence. If the lines on the disc are painted obliquely, the flashing effect appears to radiate from the centre.

Hatched lines drawn at an angle on cel will animate if hatched lines drawn at a different angle are passed behind them. This technique is useful for showing movement of flow.

Fly-up movements

Snap-action movements where items or captions suddenly appear on cue can be effected by the use of elasticated cardboard movements which fly into position when simple catches are released. The two basic movements are linear, where a card strip travels between guides, and radial, where a strip is pivoted at one end and swings round.

These diagrams need to be built in separated layers in order that the moving components can be hidden from view until released.

It is a wise policy to make the edges of the cut out portions coincide with parts of the illustration. This helps to camouflage the divisions.

Axial lighting should always be used with this type of animation as it flattens the picture and removes shadows (see page 28).

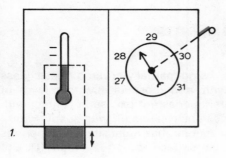

1.

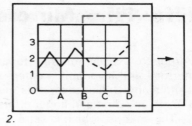

2.

3.

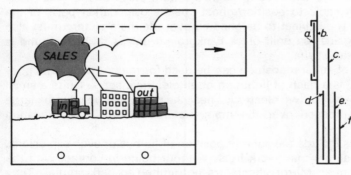

LIVE ANIMATED DIAGRAMS

1. Gauges and dials
A simple slider to demonstrate temperature, and a moving needle to indicate barometric pressure.

2. Graphs
The pull-out exposes the graph and the line is apparently drawn by an unseen hand.

3. Scenes and slogans
A combination of slider and jump-up actions provides slick animation without the necessity for pre-filming. a, 'Sales' pull-out. b, Background. c, Building. d, Boxes. e, Vehicle. f, Foreground.

Fifty-Fifty Mirrors

Although usually referred to as being partially-silvered these glass mirrors are invariably coated with a microscopically thin layer of aluminium. Unlike silver, this material does not oxidise in contact with the air, and dust and finger prints can be cleaned off with soapy water.

The coating, which is semi-transparent, has a density which permits fifty percent of the light striking the surface to be reflected back and fifty percent to pass through.

These mirrors are principally used for superimposition or 'ghost' effects where it is desired to record the effect on a single TV or film camera. One of the main advantages is that results can be seen in the camera viewfinder without waiting for later processing or tape editing.

Ghost Effects

With the mirror placed in front of the camera lens, but angled at 45°, the scene to the side of the camera is recorded together with the normal view. Similarly the mirror can be tilted up or down to record something above or below the camera.

To make a ghost image appear it is necessary to illuminate it to the same degree as the main scene. However, as the effect is that of seeing *two* subjects superimposed, both will appear to be transparent, with the light parts of one showing through the dark parts of the other. It is therefore advisable to position ghost images over darker parts of the main scene. The subject to be ghosted over the main picture must also be placed against an unlit black background unless its background is required in the scene.

This type of superimposition can be used for many things. One popular example is a flash of lightning or an electrical spark. Quite a small spark fired between two electrodes near the camera appears to be large when superimposed over the main picture of, say, a Frankenstein laboratory.

Other uses include the superimposition of flames or even explosions. In this way actors may work freely without being in contact with the source of danger. Mirror effects are not limited to dark studios. They may be used outdoors if the superimposed element can be contained in a light-tight box.

Axial Lighting

Positioned in front of the camera, a fifty-fifty mirror (or even a plain sheet of glass) may be used to provide axial lighting. This is light which travels along the axis of the camera lens. The advantage of axial lighting is that it gives flat overall lighting and that all shadows of three dimensional objects are eliminated. This is essential when using paper captions or animations of the type discussed on page 26.

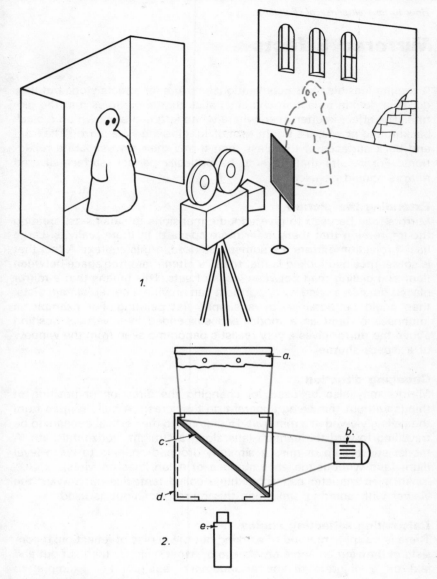

1.

a.

b.

c.

d.

e.

2.

FIFTY/FIFTY MIRRORS

1. Ghosts and apparitions

A semi-transparent mirror placed at forty-five degrees to the camera axis reflects the picture it 'sees' back into the camera lens. This second picture is therefore superimposed over the original picture and appears to be part of it. Useful for ghost shots and materialisations.

2. Axial lighting

A box with suitable cut-outs on three sides allows light, beamed in from one side, to travel along the axial path of the camera lens. An object illuminated in this fashion appears to have no shadows. a, Three-dimensional caption as model. b, Lamp. c, Semi-transparent mirror or sheet of glass. d, Black box. e, Camera.

Mirrored Effects

It is quite feasible to use conventional mirrors for effects work, but they do have double reflection characteristics that sometimes mar the picture. The effect is often seen where white letters are shown on a black background or where a bright spot of light is seen via a mirror. The front and back surfaces of the glass then throw their own separate reflections. For results that have to be optically perfect, surface-silvered mirrors should be used.

Extending the picture

Mirrors may be used to give added dimensions to small sets, creating the impression that there is far more space than there really is. Large back projection mirrors are sometimes used in this context. A fact that is sometimes overlooked is that there is often more free space between floor and ceiling than between walls of sets. This means that a mirror placed outside a window or porthole can provide a better 'distant vista' than could be obtained by a simple, flat painting. For example, a 'moonscape' built as a model and suspended in a vertical position above the mirror gives a very realistic panorama seen from the window of a 'space-shuttle'.

Changing direction

Mirrors may also be used for changing the direction or position of things without this being apparent on the screen. A ball dropped from the ceiling viewed in a mirror at 45 degrees to the vertical appears to be travelling toward the camera lens along a straight, horizontal path. A model space ship or missile similarly dropped appears to be in level flight (and without the encumbrance of nylon lines or wires).

An alien monster can shoot huge coiled tentacles out toward the viewer with unerring aim when this mirror technique is used.

Calculating reflecting angles

There is a simple method of working out the angles of reflection. It consists of drawing an angle on a piece of paper which is then cut out and laid on a diagram of the arrangement required. For example, to calculate the position and size of mirror for a back projection layout the horizontal angle of the lens must be drawn on paper and cut out as a narrow triangle. Laid over a plan of the screen so that the outer lines touch the edges of the screen the paper can now be folded anywhere along its length to show where the projector may be situated and where the mirror should be. It also shows the angle for the mirror and its horizontal width. This technique may be used for all mirror calculations including the design of periscopes and similar optical devices.

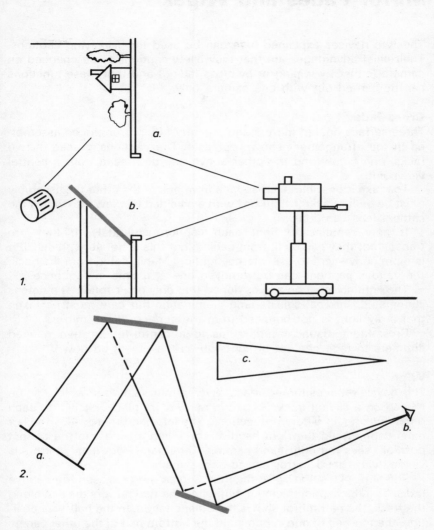

MIRRORED EFFECTS

1. Space saving
Where space is limited, scenes may be extended by using mirrors. In this example a model fastened to the back of a flat (a) appears to be on level ground outside the window (b).

2. Calculating angles
A triangular piece of paper (c) representing the angle-of-view can be folded anywhere along its length to demonstrate the angles of reflection. Folded as shown here it indicates not only the angles of the mirrors but also their sizes to see picture (a) from viewpoint (b).

Mirror Fades and Wipes

The two devices explained here can be used for displaying captions. Their chief advantages are that they allow captions to be changed on camera (either by wiping or by cross fading) and that these functions can be carried out with one camera only.

Cross-fade

Three surface-coated mirrors and one fifty-fifty mirror can be assembled in the arrangement shown opposite. The captions, placed in two racks, one below and the other above, are both seen from a central viewpoint.

To make it possible to cross-fade from one to the other the assembly must be built in a light-tight box with a shielded window into which the camera lens can 'look'.

It now remains to light each caption separately. If they are transparent they can be lit from behind, but this is not very practical. It is more convenient to use internal lighting. Manipulated from the back, the various captions can be removed one at a time in sequence.

The lighting must be so positioned that only one caption at a time is illuminated. Internal shields limit illumination but care must be taken that stray light is not bounced from the surface of the mirrors.

Cross-fading is achieved by using a centre-fed or two ganged dimmers to fade one set of lights up as the others go down.

Wipe

This device requires three surface-silvered mirrors, two of which can be moved on a sliding track. Two long mirrors are placed at 90° to each other 'looking' in different directions. The left-hand mirror sees the left hand caption and the right-hand mirror, when moved into the correct position, sees the right-hand caption. The image from these mirrors is viewed via a third mirror placed above them.

The principle is that while the front angled mirror is seen from above it displays the caption facing it, but when the two mirrors are slid along the track, the rear mirror shows the other caption. In the half-way position, the top-half of one caption and the bottom half of the other can be seen, split by an unsharp line.

Movement back and forth of the two mirrors gives a satisfactory 'wipe' from one to the other. If the captions are in packs, they can be changed alternatively from side to side giving the facility of sequential changing on one camera.

Internal illumination is a simple matter as both captions are always lit.

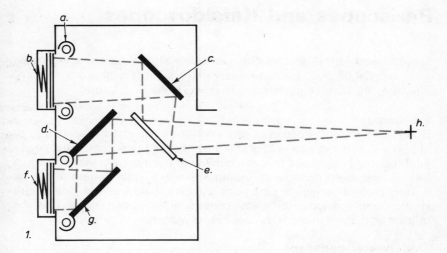

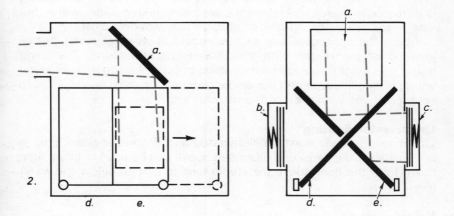

MIRROR FADES AND WIPES

1. Cross fading captions

A caption device that cross-fades from one caption to another when internal strip lights are alternately dimmed and brightened. a, Strip lights. b, Caption holder. c, d, g, Mirrors. e, Semi-transparent mirror. f, Caption holder. h, Viewpoint.

2. Wiping captions

A caption device that wipes from one caption to another. By sliding the two mirrors (d) and (e) the captions (b) and (c) are seen alternately via mirror (a).

Periscopes and Kaleidoscopes

Mirrors used in the devices outlined below should be surface-silvered on $\frac{1}{4}$ in polished plate glass. Ordinary mirrors not only give a double image, but the thinner glass distorts when fixed in a frame.

Periscope
Bulky TV and movie cameras can seldom be mounted low enough to obtain a 'worm's-eye view'. For this sort of shot a periscope must be used. Mounted in front of the lens it can lower the apparent viewpoint to a few inches above floor level. Clamped firmly to the camera it can be moved around to give a variety of tracking, panning and even zoom shots. Simple wooden or metal constructions suffice as long as the mirrors and their mountings are free of vibration.

Underwater periscope
A version of the periscope can be used to obtain underwater shots. This is particularly useful where models are being filmed under water, but where no camera diving-bell or observation windows exist.

Again, the periscope may be constructed of wood or metal, but all joints must be treated with a waterproofing compound. The lower mirror port must be covered with a sheet of plate glass to prevent water entering the periscope and the whole construction must be weighted to counteract the buoyancy of the internal air.

Underwater lighting
Underwater scenes must be illuminated and if a water-proof lamp is not available, the periscope described above can be used to beam light down from the floor above the studio tank to a point below the water level.

Kaleidoscope
Three long mirrors fastened together in the form of a triangle provide the basis of the kaleidoscope. This has a variety of caption and novelty uses.

A kaleidoscope for caption purposes can be built above a turntable and viewed through a mirror placed above.

Discs or pictures rotated below the device produce a circular composition divided into four parts, each alternate part rotating in the opposite direction to its neighbours.

Another means of using the kaleidoscope is to fix it directly to the camera lens and to view the scene in front, the composite images giving an unusual effect.

This effect is not limited to that of the three mirror combination. A tube of reflective material fastened to the camera lens surrounds the main picture with a fantasy vignette of colours and shapes.

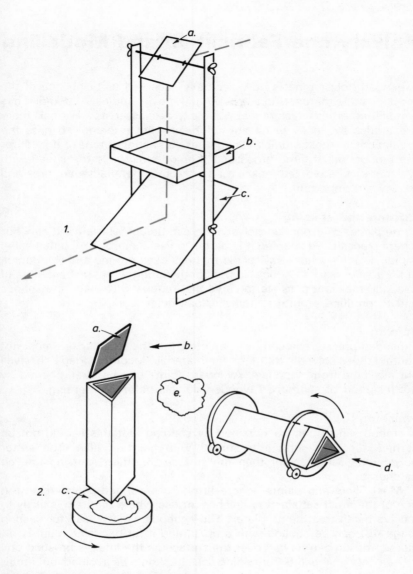

PERISCOPES AND KALEIDOSCOPES

1. Periscope

A periscope-device with adjustable mirrors. This may be used as a conventional periscope to get low angle shots, but when the glass-bottomed tray is brought into use it may be used for trick shots and special effects work. Water rippled in the tray gives a break-up effect. Pictures or models laid on the glass can be combined with the main picture. a, Small adjustable mirror. b, Glass-bottomed tray. c, Large adjustable mirror.

2. Kaleidoscope

Two applications of the three-mirror kaleidoscope. a, Mirror. b, Viewpoint. c, Revolving caption. d, Viewpoint. e, Scene.

Polystyrene Fabrication and Modelling

Expanded polystyrene is now generally accepted as being one of the most versatile materials in use in TV and movie studios. Although it has certain properties which render it liable to be classed as a fire-risk, there are grades available which are sufficiently fire retardant to pass the regulations in most studios. Its lightness and strength make it ideal for the production of large props and scenic items while the speed with which it can be worked makes it an attractive material where time and money are important.

Cutting and shaping
Large pieces of expanded-polystyrene can be cut with a hand saw but where pieces need shaping it is better to use a sharp thin-bladed knife. An ideal tool is a hack-saw blade that has been ground and sharpened, but it is necessary to hone this frequently during work. A sharp knife of this kind makes it possible to carve the material into elaborate shapes and to produce sculptural items or bas relief work.

Joining
Expanded polystyrene can be cemented, but the glue chosen must not contain those solvents that melt the material. Recommended adhesives are available from suppliers. Awkward joints can be strengthened by the insertion of sharpened wooden dowels before cementing.

Finishing
A smooth finish can be obtained by sanding, but this should not be carried out after surface treatment with paint or filler. The softer polystyrene sands faster than the surface treatment causing uneven patches to appear.

Most fillers and paints adhere firmly to expanded-polystyrene, but one of the most satisfactory finishes for use where the item is likely to receive harsh treatment is latex. The aqueous variety used for casting (page 46) can be applied with a brush and if further reinforcing is required, muslin can be laid over the surface as the latex is brushed on.

Aerosol spray paints containing solvent should be avoided, but emulsion paint works well.

For the production of rocks, chunks of polystyrene can be burnt with a flame torch. The surface melts, creating a rough cratered effect closely resembling rock or stone. This treatment gives the material a hard, glazed texture, more brittle than the normal expanded polystyrene. WARNING: All such work must be done in the open air and every precaution taken against breathing the fumes.

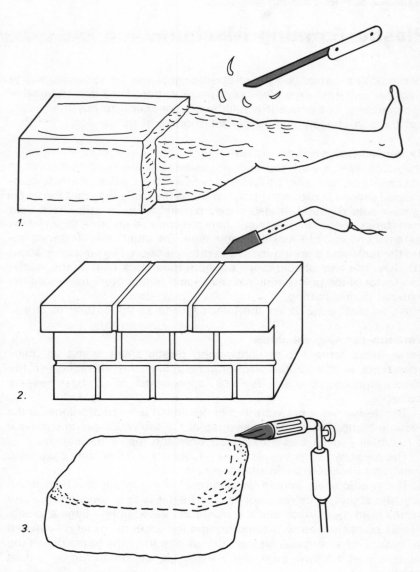

EXPANDED POLYSTYRENE

1. Shaping
Expanded polystyrene may be shaped with a sharp, thin-bladed knife that is kept constantly honed.

2. Patterns
Patterns may be engraved with a hot iron.

3. Forming
Hard stony surfaces can be imitated by melting the surface with a blowtorch. Where heat is applied to this material the fumes should not be inhaled.

Plastic Forming Machines.

Two machines which aid the effects designer are the vacuum-forming machine and the expanded-polystyrene cutter. They are obtainable commercially, but where it would be uneconomical to buy them, they can be built cheaply and simply for short-term usage.

Expanded-polystyrene cutter

This comprises a work-top and an overhead beam which supports an electrically heated wire. Its function is to aid the cutting of small, complicated shapes in expanded-polystyrene in the same way that the fret or jig-saw cuts plywood. It also allows parallel slices or strips to be cut from block material. The work bench supports an arm to which is fastened one end of a nickel-chrome wire. The other end is fastened under the table and is spring-loaded to retain tension. The voltage is about 20–30v. The wire should reach no more than black heat as the insulation factor of the polystyrene causes a rapid temperature rise inside the material during cutting.

An adjustable guide on the bench facilitates the cutting of strips.

Vacuum-forming machine

Small items formed from lightweight, plastic sheet speed up many operations in the property-making field and the versatility of the vacuum-forming process is well appreciated in a busy effects workshop.

The device has a flat work-top under which is fitted a cylinder and a vacuum pump. The cylinder has a tap at the top which permits it, once it is partially exhausted, to suck air from the top of the bench.

The other two components are a double frame for holding the plastic sheet and an electrical heating-element.

The plastic sheet should be clamped in the frame and held down over the object to be reproduced. The heater is then lowered to a few inches from the surface and the plastic is heated until it begins to sag. At this point the heater is removed and the vacuum vessel is switched to 'suck'. The air exhausting from the lower part of the frame draws the heated plastic down onto the master object, producing a faithful reproduction.

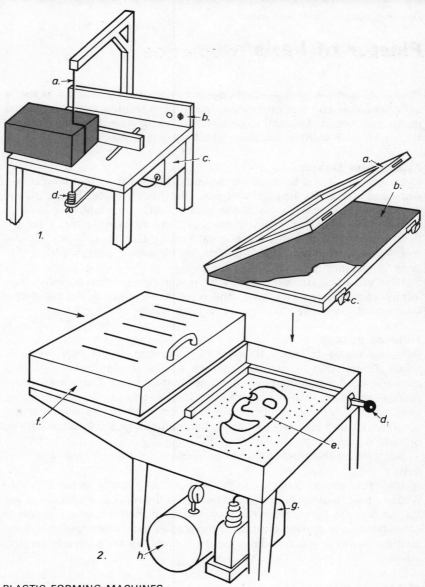

PLASTIC FORMING MACHINES

1. Hot-wire cutting
A table with a tensioned hot wire used to cut slices from blocks of expanded polystyrene. It may also be used to cut patterns in sheet material. a, Hot wire. b, Switch and indicator lamp. c, Low-voltage transformer. d, Tension spring.

2. Forming sheet plastic
Plastic sheet held in a rectangular clamp is heated until it becomes pliable. It is then drawn down by suction onto a master where it cools and forms a rigid copy of the original. a, Frame. b, Plastic sheet. c, Clamp. d, Vacuum control. e, Master. f, Movable heater. g, Vacuum pump. h, Vacuum cylinder.

Plaster of Paris

Plaster of paris is used extensively in movie and TV studios. It has a variety of uses and few other materials are as versatile. It is used for the making of moulds for casting glass-fibre and resins and is also used for the making of statues, breaking crockery and scenic items.

Mixing the plaster

Plaster must always be added to water and never the other way about. Assess the quantity needed and pour that much water into a plastic bowl. Then, using a cup, add the plaster until dry material builds up above the level of the water. At this point stir thoroughly until a lump--free, smooth, creamy mixture results. Test by dipping a finger into the mix. When withdrawn, the finger should be evenly coated with a thin creamy plaster.

Well mixed plaster sets quickly, so it is important that no more than is required is mixed at a time. The residue that sets in the bowl can, when hard, be broken out by flexing the bowl.

Release agents

Plaster adheres to many things and, of course, sticks very firmly to other plaster. If it is required to take a plaster reproduction from a plaster mould a suitable release agent must be used. There are several proprietary substances available, but for general use shellac may be used to coat the mould. This should be done when the mould is ab-solutely dry and two or even three thin coats are usually necessary to provide a good seal.

Before use, the shellac should be given a light brush over with wax polish.

Clay also acts as a barrier to prevent plaster sticking to plaster. Thin walls or fences of clay are used to delineate the halves of a mould when it is being cast. Sometimes the clay is used in the form of strips and at other times it is applied directly to the plaster as a diluted wash. Thinn-ed down with water and brushed on it provides an adequate parting agent.

Miscellaneous

To accelerate the setting of plaster add a little alum to the water before the mixing process.

To slow down the setting time add a small amount of size to the water. Stale beer also works well.

If plaster is worked continuously instead of allowing it to set and harden the resultant 'killed' mixture provides a good material for repair-ing damaged plaster work. It can be pressed into holes and cracks with a thin bladed knife and sanded when dry.

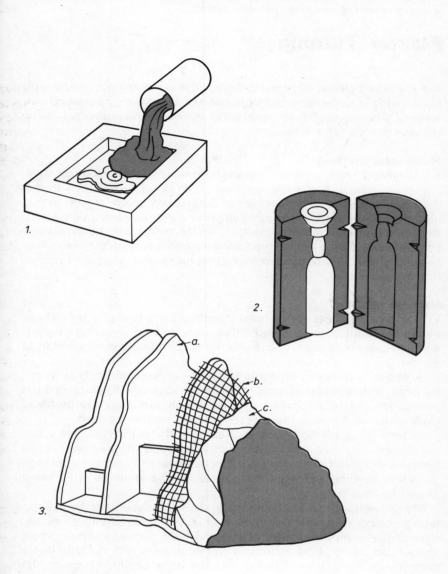

PLASTER OF PARIS

1. Open moulds
Plaster of paris is used for casting objects in open moulds. These moulds are usually flexible to facilitate removal of the cast.

2. Plaster moulds
Plaster is also used to make moulds from which flexible articles are cast.

3. Scenic items
Plaster applied to scrim or open-weave cloth is often used in the construction of such scenic items as rocks. a, Timber. b, Wire netting. c, Cloth.

Plaster Turning

Freshly mixed plaster of paris hardens within a few minutes and during that time it is possible to model it into regular shapes by pouring and turning. This is useful for producing cylindrical or spherical items without the use of a lathe.

Horizontal method
A horizontal spindle on which has been securely fastened some anchoring material (such as cloth or bandage) is laid in two vee-shaped stocks. A shaped metal profile is then fixed in a suitable position (angled so that wet plaster will run back from its edge) and the plaster is poured onto the spindle while it is slowly rotated. As the wet plaster builds up it is scraped away by the profile, producing a smooth and uniform item. This method is useful for making master items for the moulding or vacuum-- forming processes.

Vertical method
Where large and heavy amounts of plaster are involved it is not so easy to use the rotating spindle method. An alternative is to perform the action vertically, with a rotating profile working around a static amount of plaster.

A vertically-mounted tube fitted firmly to a baseboard acts as a centre point. In this is placed a rod, to the top end of which is attached the profile. The plaster is poured onto the baseboard while the profile is slowly rotated, forming the object from the bottom upward.

In both these methods fluid plaster cleared away by the profile can be scooped up and re-poured over the article. Where very large amounts of plaster are being used it is necessary to stop the operation from time to time and mix fresh plaster. At this stage all dried swarf should be cleared away.

When large articles are being made the centre mass can be built up with pieces of expanded polystyrene or other coarse filler material, using the plaster only for the outer layer. With the vertical method female shapes can be turned if a strong supporting outer wall is made to accommodate the plaster. Turning must be done carefully because the fluid material runs to the bottom and has to be scooped out as the work progresses.

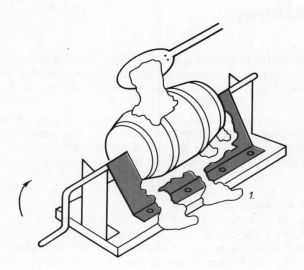

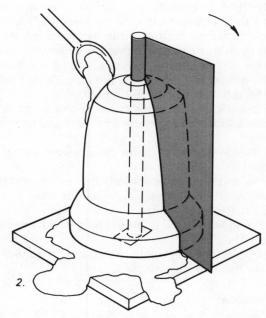

PLASTER TURNING

1. Revolving spindle
A method of using liquid plaster to create a barrel shaped object. The object is revolved against a stationary profile.

2. Revolving profile
To form a large plaster bell, the profile is revolved while the object is held stationary.

Mould Making

Plaster moulds used for the reproduction of items in resin, wax or latex are either open moulds for straightforward pouring or enclosed (piece) moulds comprising two or more interlocking pieces used for swilling or casting.

Flexible moulds, usually backed with plaster supporting-cradles and known as 'case' moulds are used for laying up glass-fibre objects or for casting complicated items where there are problems connected with undercuts or detail that could not be withdrawn from an inflexible plaster mould.

How to make a two-piece mould

Place the master to be moulded on a flat board and surround half of it with clay. Finish the edge of the clay cleanly and uniformly around the master to provide a firm support for the top half of the mould.

Using a cup, pour the freshly mixed plaster over the item until a thin coat has completely covered the surface. Repeat this action several times until a thick and uniform coat has been built up over the master.

Endeavour to flatten the top of the mould with a tool as the pouring progresses, so that it can stand steadily when you turn it over for the next operation. Allow plaster to harden and clean tools and utensils.

Invert the mould and remove all the clay. *Do not* disturb the master embedded in the first half of the mould.

Using a sharp knife, cut three tapering 'vee' slots in the edge of the mould. These will act as registers when the two halves come together for moulding.

Using a diluted clay wash, paint the edge where the second half will meet the first.

Repeat the first pouring operation until the second half has built up.

Allow plenty of time for plaster to harden then separate the mould and remove the master item.

Cut a pouring hole in the edge of one of the halves where it will not mar the reproduction.

Keep the halves of the mould together with adhesive tape or string and write on the outside what it is.

Flexible moulds

These may be cast in various proprietary materials or even in a strong size solution prepared by dissolving size or Scotch glue in hot water. It sets like a firm jelly.

When pouring moulding material over a master item it is important to pour to one side so that the material rises around the item. This prevents air bubbles being trapped in the detail.

44

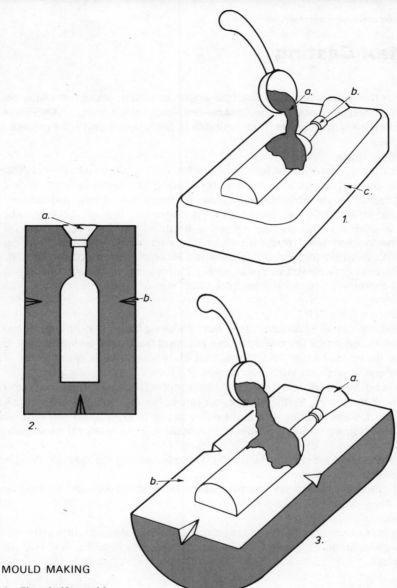

MOULD MAKING

1. First half-mould
The master is embedded in a block of clay and plaster is poured over it to form one half of the mould. a, Plaster. b, Master. c, Clay.

2. Preparing the mould
The poured half of the plaster mould. The clay has been removed and the master now lies embedded in plaster. Locator notches are cut, and a clay plug formed for the pouring hole. a, Clay plug. b, Locator notches.

3. Second half-mould
Plaster is poured on to a clay wash on the first half and flows into the locator notches to form an interlocking second mould. a, Clay plug. b, Clay wash.

Latex Casting

One of the most versatile materials, aqueous-based, liquid latex may be poured into moulds to reproduce all sorts of property items and costume embellishments. It is available in both heavy and light grades.

Casting latex
Poured into plaster moulds, latex adheres to the walls, whereupon the water content soaks into the plaster leaving the latex behind.

Moulds should have their internal surfaces clean, dry and uncontaminated with release agents. Latex is poured in through a convenient hole and after being swilled around is emptied out. This action should be repeated at least three times at intervals of 30 minutes allowing each application to thoroughly coat the internal surface of the mould.

The cast may be left to dry naturally, but it is more convenient to put it in a moderate oven. The heat cures the latex and dries out the mould.

Grade
The heavy grade of casting latex may be used for making many items ranging from mock armour to sticks and iron bars used in fight scenes. Latex items have the advantage that they can take a great deal of punishment without suffering damage.

The lighter grade may be used in the construction of face-masks to be worn by actors. With eye and mouth holes cut out, the latex mask can, by the application of make-up, be made to blend into the natural face to a degree where it is almost impossible to tell where the joins occur.

Another use for the lighter grade is in the making of insects, animals and medical specimens.

Vegetables, meats and fish can also be cast easily and cheaply.

Finish
Latex can be coloured with most paints and enamels and even with varnishes and lacquers. These finishes crack if severely handled, but seldom flake off.

Other uses
Applied with a brush, latex painted over expanded polystyrene gives it a hard resilient coating that is useful for artificial bricks and rocks.

Bandage wound round an actor's leg and coated with latex can be cut off when dry and used later as a simulated plaster cast.

A puddle of latex poured onto a sheet of glass and allowed to dry may be painted to resemble oil, paint, molasses etc. Laid on the floor in the studio it looks real without being messy. Useful for applying to cookers, expensive rented furniture, carpets etc.

LATEX CASTING

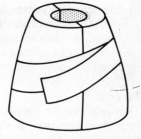

Latex is poured into a dry plaster piece mould.

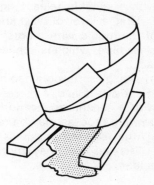

After being allowed to stand for a while the mould is inverted and drained.

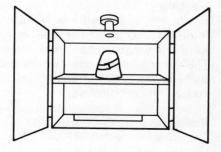

The mould is left in an oven to cure.

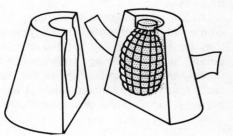

The mould is opened and the cast removed.

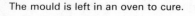
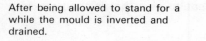

47

Glass Fibre Lay-Ups and Casting Resin

Cold-setting polyester resins usually consist of the resin, a hardener and a catalyst. When mixed, they set as a hard brittle compound. In itself the resin is not structurally tough but when combined with strands of glass fibre it produces a material which is well known for lightness and strength.

Lay-up

The best moulds for resin and glass fibre are made from latex or flexible moulding compound supported by a thick plaster backing to prevent them distorting. If a plaster-of-paris mould is used it must be treated with a suitable release agent.

First, a layer of resin known as the gel coat is applied to the surface of the mould with a brush. It is allowed to harden slightly so that the glass fibre, which is applied next, does not penetrate and spoil the surface.

The glass is obtainable either as a woven material or in chopped strands. It is laid, a piece at a time, on the gel coat, and impregnated with a second application of resin, firmly brushed into the glass. The layering process may be repeated as many times as necessary to build up the required thickness.

The gel coat may contain a pigment to give the finished article a colour.

Casting

Resin can be poured into moulds to produce cast objects. Powdered metals added to the first coat in the mould (it is wasteful to use them for the entire pour) can make the cast resin look remarkably like metal. This is useful when prop knives and weapons are being made. It is also a cheap and easy method of simulating bronze busts, brass medallions and aluminium fittings.

Finishing

The finished cast must be lightly sanded with an abrasive material. Usually 'wet and dry' paper works well. The cast should then be buffed up with a rag and metal polish as would be the case with real metal.

To improve the look of certain 'metal' casts it is possible to wipe on colours and treatments. If the article purports to be bronze, green paint may be applied to the surface and then wiped clean. The residue left behind in the low lying areas gives a satisfactory patina of age. Brown ochre for brass and graphite for steel and aluminium give equally satisfactory results. If an article is to look rusty, it should be varnished, partially wiped clean and then dusted with cocoa.

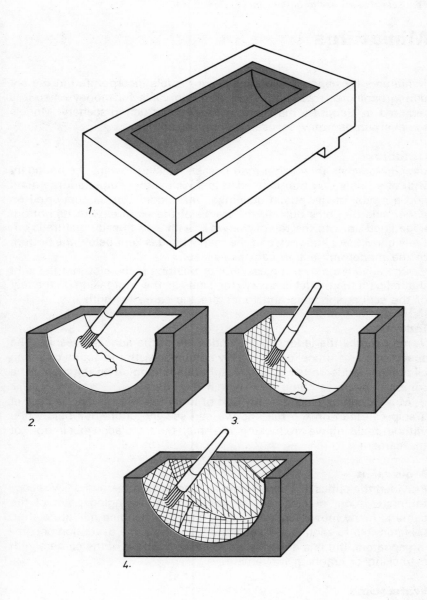

GLASS FIBRE LAY-UP

1. Case moulds — flexible moulds supported by plaster cases — are often used for glass fibre lay-ups.
2. Resin is applied to the internal surfaces of the mould and allowed to gel.
3. Glass fibre is brushed firmly onto the resin and more resin is brushed into the weave of the material.
4. Overlapping pieces are applied until the mould is covered.

Miniatures

Miniatures (or hanging miniatures) are models incorporated in the set during filming or recording. They are good value for money when it is required to elaborate the scene without constructing scenery. Models for this purpose may be used indoors or outdoors.

Outdoors

Imagine a scene in which a man is seen walking toward the boundary wall of a prison. All that is needed is a wall with a suitable foreground and a model of the prison buildings. The model can be supported on either side by poles outside the frame of the picture, with its bottom edge lined up with the top of the wall. Such a composite picture is entirely convincing and provided the man's head is kept below the bottom of the model any action can take place.

One advantage over a glass shot or painting is the fact that the light that falls on the model is always the same as the light falling on the rest of the scene; shadows and tones are the same for both.

Indoors

'A man climbs the ladder to the underside of the huge spaceship.' The space ship as a model can be easily combined with the action of a man climbing a ladder in the studio. A light beamed down on the man as he climbs appears to come from within the ship.

Models can be placed in any part of the frame. A man on the deck of a ship can lean on the rail and we can see the entire hull below him without realising we are looking at a small model, placed just in front of the camera.

Movement

Provided the optics of a camera are in line and that the film or TV receptor plate is on, or close to, the pivoting and swinging point of the camera, many movements are possible with a hanging miniature shot. It is possible to zoom and to pan and tilt without the deception becoming apparent, but it is not possible to move the base of the camera with a tracking or crabbing movement.

Waterscape

A miniature suspended above a water scene can modify the landscape beyond. For example, the horizon of the sea could be equipped with a tropical island, or, on a smaller scale, a pond could appear to be at the foot of steep cliffs. The sea shot with broken water is comparatively easy, but the surface of the pond, if unruffled, reflects what is *really* there in the background and *not* the miniature foreground cliffs.

MINIATURES

1. Hanging miniatures

Models suspended or supported in front of the camera can be made to seem part of the scene.

2. Advantages

Miniatures often give better results than glass shots. The light that falls on the main scene also illuminates the model, giving similar conditions of contrast and shadows. This technique gives greater choice of camera angles.

Model Shots

Model shots are used frequently in both film and TV productions, because they offer an economical way of obtaining certain sequences. Buildings figure prominently. It is often cheaper to make a model than search for the right house and send a crew out to film it.

Static scenic models
These are often used to establish a viewpoint. Houses, castles and landscapes are commonplace, but there are also more unusual uses for the static model shot. The 'Space City on Planet Z', the hull of the ship torn apart in the collision, the pylons of the mighty bridge showing structural failures. How else could one achieve these shots?

Action models
The simplest example is a house at night in which one window is seen to light up. The most complicated could be a ship heaving on a storm-tossed sea. It is essential to be able to assess the work and costs involved and to be able to gauge the level of success of the final recording. There is no point in making and filming something which in the end is going to look like a model shot.

Any action that can safely be recorded at normal speed (the window lighting up) can be used directly on TV, but where the action calls for crashing trains, or buildings to be blown up, the models must be pre-filmed using a high speed camera. This is so that the action can be scaled to the size of the model. The speed of action in real life has to be calculated and then multiplied by the size relationship of the model (e.g., a quarter scale model has to be filmed at four times normal speed.)

This is a rough and ready guide, because certain things do not react well when their action is slowed down. Prime examples are water and flame. Where these elements are called for it is essential to construct models as large as possible.

For model buildings on fire it is often better to employ smoke and light rather than actual flame.

Materials
Card, balsa wood, plaster and plastic-kit parts are common ingredients in model construction. If a model is static it merely has to be well finished to look convincing, but if it has to do something the action and the aftermath may determine the materials used. For example, in a fire scene the windows should not melt, nor should brick walls curl up and burn. In explosion sequences, the interior might be seen afterwards and unfinished card and wood must not be left to destroy the illusion.

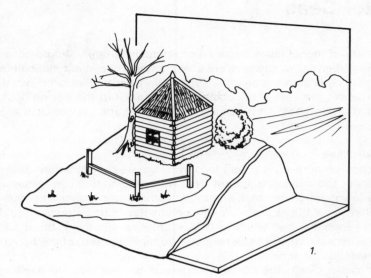

MODEL SHOTS

1. Models to set the scene
Three-dimensional models are often used to establish a scene, and in some cases they may have to be very detailed.

2. Part-model construction
It is sometimes simpler to use a photograph with only part of the model built in three dimensions. This is particularly useful if some action has to take place on what would otherwise be a complicated model.

53

Model Seas

The filming of model ships in studio or improvised tanks should not be undertaken lightly as these scenes are among the most difficult to create with satisfactory realism. Clever editing and subliminal views do much to make the best of unconvincing material, but there is no doubt that a bad model shot can destroy a dramatic situation rather than support it.

Miniature sea

A seascape comprising a placid lagoon or the view of a distant desert island is not too difficult to create. This type of miniature can be set up in a shallow plastic-lined tank erected at camera lens height and filmed in a studio. Where the script calls for complicated action, however, such as a ship foundering in a storm or a submarine surfacing, the model must be operated in a robustly constructed tank situated on the floor or in a proper studio tank.

In all cases where the scene is supposed to take place in daylight, the tank must be backed by a light sky cloth or a back projection screen. Without such an area of flat light to reflect on the surface of the water, the scene looks like a night shot.

Waves

Waves can be produced simply by paddling flat boards fixed to the ends of poles. These should be manipulated on opposite sides of the tank, the cross modulation producing credible miniature waves, but filming has to be at high speed to slow the waves down.

Horizon

In model tanks the waves must not disturb the horizon, which should of course appear as a straight line. One way of overcoming this problem is to have a sloping board at the back of the tank on which the waves spend themselves. To hide the board the tank must be kept filled with water, the overflow taking place at the back of the tank over the sloping board.

Model boats can be filmed on outdoor ponds and lakes, but in these cases, if the viewpoint is a low one, the horizon presents even more trouble. A solution may sometimes be found in putting down a layer of smoke over the water in the background. The smoke blends with the sky and gives the impression that the horizon is much lower than it really is.

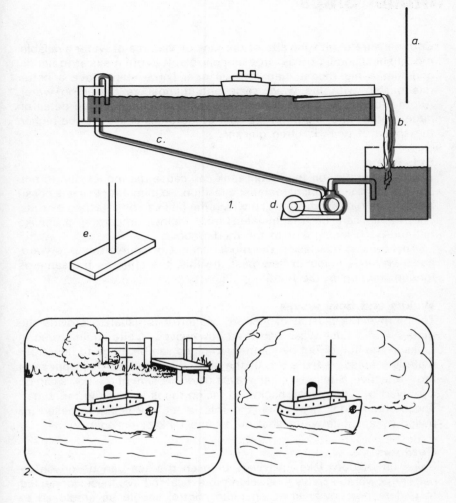

MODEL SEAS

1. Studio tank

Small tanks constructed in the studio should have one low side (the horizon) over which water can flow continuously. This hides the construction of the tank. a, Backing. b, Overflow. c, Return. d, Pump. e, Wave making paddle.

2. Hiding the background

Troublesome backgrounds can sometimes be eliminated if it is possible to lay down smoke. Blending with both water and sky this falsifies the horizon level giving the model ship a more realistic scale.

Model Ships

Commensurate with the size of the tank or the area of water available, model ships should be as large as possible. It is often easier to handle and film a big model than a small one. Large ships have a better relationship with the wave scale and manoeuvre better on water. Another bonus is that it is generally easier to construct the detail on large models and, although the cost of materials is likely to be higher, the speed of work is often quicker.

Sub-frame
Waves generated on the studio tank can cause the model ship to bob up and down in an uncharacteristic fashion. To eliminate this it is possible to construct a sub-frame to which the hull can be attached by rods. The frame can be manipulated from below, imparting a lifelike roll-and-pitch movement to the model above.

Anchored in this fasion the model cannot of course travel forward, but if water is made to flow past the hull, the effect is the same as forward motion of the boat.

Wakes and bow waves
To improve the illusion of forward motion it is usual to provide the model with a false wake and false bow-waves. White liquid stored in tanks in the hull or fed by submerged pipes can be made to flow from waterline holes at the stern of the ship, the resultant trail appearing most effective. Similarly, small waves on either side of the bows can be contrived by fixing small backward facing tubes just below the water. These effects look best when the ship is actually being propelled (or pulled by an underwater line) on a large tank or on open water.

Outdoors
Ships on outdoor lakes or rivers or even the sea can be driven by battery-powered screws. It is seldom practical to have these connected to underwater power lines, so radio control should be employed to switch the motor and to control the rudder.

It is often found that extended keels help to damp down unwanted rolling movements.

Submarine shots
'Underwater' shots of submarines can be filmed in the dry if the models are hung on wires in front of a green background. Careful lighting can create the illusion that the vessel is actually under water, particularly if a water ripple effect is projected on the upper part of the backing and onto the submarine itself.

Another method is to use the model against front or rear scenic projection of an underwater setting.

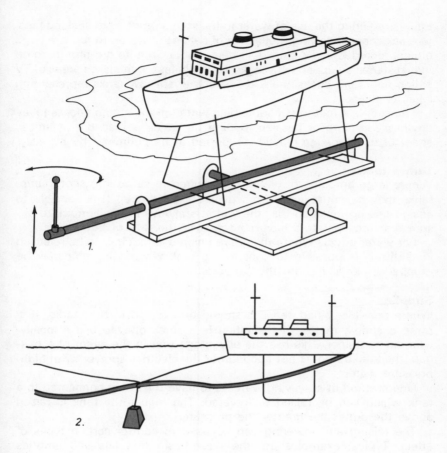

MODEL SHIPS

1. Storm sequences
Model ships appearing in storm sequences are best anchored to a fixed base which can be manipulated to impart a realistic pitch and roll action.

2. Towing precautions
Models being towed should have their tow lines weighted to keep them below water level. Extended keels reduce unnatural motion caused by the towing action. Take care that the wake from the towing vessel does not appear in the shot.

Water in the Studio

Effects requiring the use of water in the studio range from 'leaking taps' to epic scenes involving thousands of gallons of water. Rarely are large effects recorded in TV studios, it being more usual to pre-film them on movie stages equipped with tanks. Nevertheless, quite large areas of TV stuido floors are occasionally dressed with shallow tanks representing lakes or rivers.

The simplest method of containing water on the studio floor is to lay down scene cloth or hessian (burlap) on which is placed a seamless sheet of heavy-gauge plastic, supported at its perimeter by planks.

Dump tanks

Where large amounts of water are required to surge into shot, dump-tanks may be constructed from plastic lined timber. It is sensible to design tipping-tanks so that the water is always in equilibrium, to ensure that the operators have control over the rate of flow.

For water effects where the entire volume is required to be released instantly, it is possible to construct a tank where one side may be dropped by knocking out the supports.

Supplies

Where possible, piped services should be avoided in the studio. It is often a simple matter, if the effect is a small one, to use a locally-situated container. This has the advantage that in the event of a mishap, the studio floor is not flooded nor the electrics sprayed with high-pressure water.

One method of supplying water is to have the effect connected to a tank which can be raised or lowered. The higher the tank is raised above the outlet the greater the pressure.

The raising and lowering can be used to control certain types of effect. Typical examples are the wash-basin that fills and empties through the plug-hole and the glass indicator tube in which the liquid rises and falls.

Where a high-pressure squirting action is required, it is often convenient to use the compressed-air type of fire extinguisher. This should be filled to two-thirds of its capacity with water and then pressurised either with an airline or foot-pump.

Ornamental fountains

Conventional pumps and sprays may be used for ornamental fountains in the studio, but the sound of tinkling water often becomes a distraction. To overcome this, the bowl should be lined with felt cloth and the water allowed to drain into a lower receptacle.

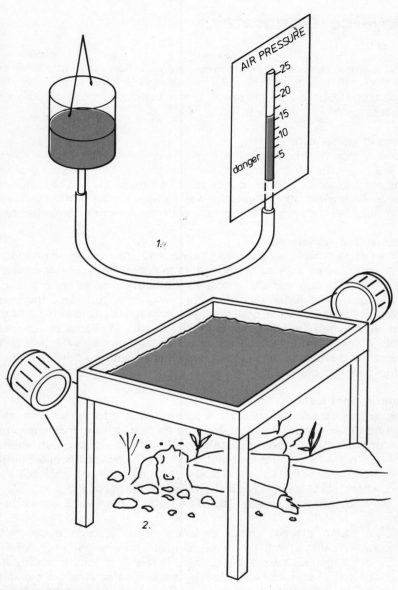

WATER IN THE STUDIO

1. Simulated gauges
The raising and lowering of a water container behind the scenes allows a water-tube gauge to be controlled to very fine limits.

2. Using water trays
A 'drowned person' sequence may be filmed using the real actor if he or she is situated underneath a glass bottomed tray containing water.

Dry-Ice Generators

The swirling clouds of white mist used for 'dream sequences' are produced by immersing solid carbon dioxide (dry ice) in hot water. The resulting clouds are a mixture of water vapour and liberated carbon dioxide gas.

Simple generation
Solid carbon dioxide is supplied in conveniently-sized blocks that can be broken up with a hammer. Dropped into hot water the pieces produce copious clouds of vapour, but in doing so make an audible bubbling noise. As it gives off its heat, the water quickly cools and turns to ice. The effect diminishes in proportion with the lowering temperature.

Controlled generation
A well designed and constructed generator avoids cooling-off problems. The water is heated electrically and its temperature is thermostatically maintained throughout the operation. Generation takes place within a box with good thermal insulation that also helps to reduce the noise level. The broken dry ice, contained in a wire basket, is lowered into the hot water when the effect is required. Lifting it out causes the effect to stop. A small fan positioned above water level can be switched on to assist the distribution of the mist, which is sometimes ducted away in large-bore flexible pipes.

Operational notes
The water vapour eventually condenses back into water. The area around the generator can therefore get quite wet if the machine is run for long periods. Carbon dioxide is not a poisonous gas, but when it collects in low lying areas it excludes the air. The possibility of asphyxiation must be anticipated where scenes include low-lying enclosed sets and where performers have to lie down in the mist.

Very hot water causes the clouds to rise. Cooler water keeps them down.

Live steam played across broken dry ice also produces mist. Generators using steam are much simpler and cheaper to make.

Where large areas are being covered in mist it is helpful to surround the area with two-foot-high retaining walls. Scenic flats are suitable.

Some attention should be paid to the necessity for siting dry ice generators where they can replenish the effect with the minimum of intrusion. The fairy glade loses its aura of quiet enchantment if dry ice clouds can be seen belting in from one side of the set. Sympathetic direction can help if cameras pick out different parts of the set while others are being replenished.

Dry ice should not be handled with bare hands.

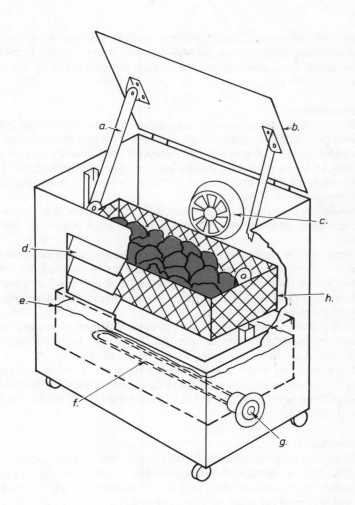

DRY ICE GENERATOR

A typical dry-ice machine used in film and television studios. a, Lowering arm. b, Operating lid. c, Booster fan (use optional). d, Outlet louvres. e, Thermally-insulated water trough. f, Water heater. g, Thermostat. h, Wire basket containing broken dry ice.

Radar and Oscilloscopes

A practical commercial radar display requires a signal from a rotating aerial to produce a picture on the cathode-ray tube. It is, therefore, seldom possible to use fully practical radar equipment in studio productions.

Radar scanner
To simulate a working radar it is possible to have a 'display' which is scanned by a rotating radial 'beam' of light. This can be achieved by using a rotating disc of clear plastic sprayed with black paint in such a way that it fades gradually from clear to opaque. The opaque section should cover at least one third of the disc, while the clear area should be in the form of a narrow line.

The disc is fitted to the extended spindle of a gear box driven by an electric motor. Alternatively it can be driven by a motor via belts and pulleys.

In front of the disc is the display. This is also a sheet of clear plastic sprayed uniformly with black paint to render it opaque. The display (usually in the form of a map) is scratched through the paint leaving a clear, brilliant outline. Next comes a sheet of tracing paper and finally another sheet of clear plastic.

A light placed behind the disc provides a typical rotational scan followed by the characteristic fade out. The effect is enhanced by putting a yellow or blue-green gel in front of the display.

Where 'moving' blips are required a number of clear areas can be covered and uncovered in turn by pulling sliders behind the main display disc. This activity is carried out during the period when the area is blacked out.

Oscillographs
Oscilloscope patterns, provided that they do not have to show varying patterns, can be simulated with a double mirror partially sprayed on both sides with black paint. The paint is sprayed in such a way as to fade out the trailing edge of both mirrors.

A light reflecting from the rotating mirrors falls on a display which has been prepared by spraying clear plastic with black paint and then scratching out the area required for the simulated trace. The front is covered with tracing paper and coloured gel.

Mock traces
A motorised, revolving bent wire, painted white and set in a black hole gives the impression of a realistic trace if not seen too closely. A useful gimmick for science-fiiction sets.

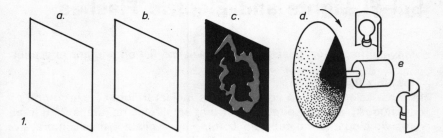

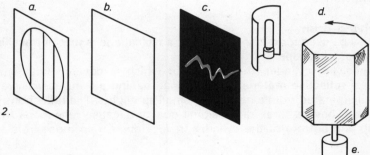

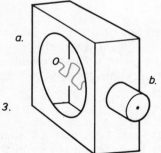

RADAR AND OSCILLOSCOPES

1. Parts for a motorised radar scan simulator.
a, Clear plastic front. b, Diffuser screen. c, Clear plastic with scan pattern. d, Graduated disc. e, Motor.

2. Parts for a simulated oscilloscope display.
a, Clear plastic front. b, Diffuser screen. c, Clear plastic with trace pattern. d, Mirror drum. e, Motor.

3. A 'busy' display to use in the background.
a, White painted bent wire in black box. b, Motor.

63

Sci-Fi Lights and Electric Flashes

Many lighting effects can be used in science-fiction and horror scenes.

Flashing lights

In most science-fiction control rooms indicator lights flash on and off continuously and, despite the fact that small electric lamps with internal-switching thermostats are commonly available, these impressive scenes are often expensive and complicated.

An alternative is to illuminate from behind, via revolving mirrors, a fascia-panel containing punched out holes backed by coloured gel.

A second method, where the display is for background use only, is to hang large reflective sequins on thread and to agitate them gently with air from a fan.

Revolving drum

This may be used for many effects, but a typical one is that of travelling through a star-scape.

A revolving cylinder, the surface of which is covered with small pieces of reflective material, is positioned behind a translucent screen and is illuminated from a number of small spotlights. The reflections on the screen have a three-dimensional quality because reflections from the top and bottom of the cylinder travel slower than those from the front.

Rotating disc

A disc of clear, acrylic plastic rotated in front of a camera lens can produce many effects. Heated and bent it gives a water-shimmering effect. Painted with radial black stripes it gives a flicker effect and painted with white blobs that reflect light back into the lens, it gives a flashing effect.

Electric spark

A large-capacity, high-voltage spark coil, can flash six-inch sparks between electrodes for super-imposition on studio scenes in a way that makes the sparks appear to occur between other objects. For maximum effect the electrodes should be housed in a black-painted box with a single frontal aperture into which the camera looks. Many variations of spark can be produced by using different electrodes. A single-point electrode positioned in the centre of a circular electrode produces sparks that radiate in all directions. A sheet of patterned glass or plastic sprinkled with iron-fillings can be placed between the electrodes to give a multi-spark effect.

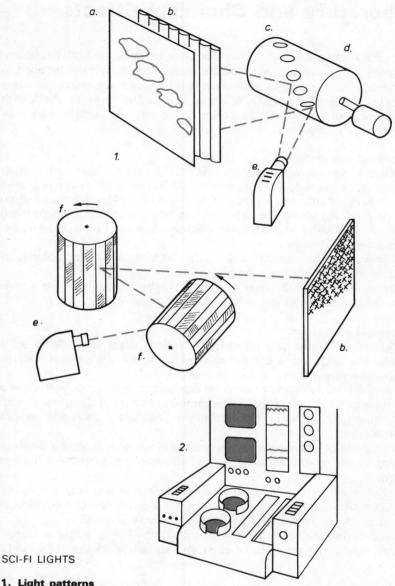

SCI-FI LIGHTS

1. Light patterns
The light from a projector can be attenuated in many ways to form interesting light patterns that can be used to dress space-ship interiors and sci-fi laboratories. a, Diffuser screen. b, Patterned glass. c, Plastic mirror discs. d, Revolving drum. e, Projector. f, Mirror drum.

2. Sci-fi control panel
Directed on to screen material positioned behind cut-out fascia panels the light patterns make the whole scene appear busy and interesting.

Laboratory and Chemical Effects

Laboratory sets are either comedic or semi-practical. In both cases, unless they are required simply for dressing, something must be seen to happen. In the comedy arrangement it is usually sufficient to fill a few chemical flasks with brightly coloured liquids and to prime them with small pieces of dry ice prior to a take. But for implied realism more subtle effects are required.

Chemical equipment

A suitable arrangement of chemical flasks, glass tubes and rubber hoses can be made to work automatically if a piece of dry-ice is placed in a flask of warm water connected to the system. The released carbon dioxide bubbling along the various glass tubes makes the whole thing appear busy. Colouring of the water in the tubes can be achieved by using soluble food dyes.

Compressed air introduced into the bottom of a glass column of liquid gives an impressive bubble display.

Steam from a small boiler or electric kettle conducted over a container of dry-ice gives the effect of acid fumes leaking away.

Chemical reactions

Carbon tetrachloride poured onto expanded polystyrene dissolves it rapidly. The polystyrene can be finished to resemble such materials as paper, minerals, metals, wood or even flesh.

Titanium tetrachloride poured on clothing or thrown on a floor in a test tube or flask fumes rapidly, resembling the most dangerous acid.

By mixing acetic acid with cyclohexylamine, fumes are produced that resemble light smoke or 'steam'.

A solution of potassium permanganate in water produces a browny-mauve liquid (not unlike some wines). It clears if a solution of hypo is added.

Invisible writing or marks on paper or cloth appear on cue if they are written with a solution of sodium salicylate. Application of a solution of iron sulphate or ferric chloride turns the marks brown.

Most carbonated soft drinks fizz animatedly if free sugar is added.

Solutions of bicarbonate of soda and tartaric acid foam if mixed.

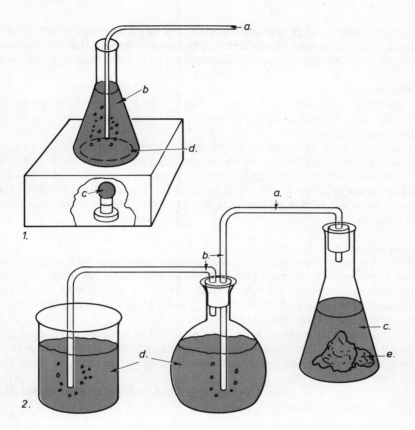

LABORATORY AND CHEMICAL EFFECTS

1. Bubbles
Compressed air blown into a flask makes an impressive bubble display. a, Compressed
air. b, Coloured liquid. c, Lamp. d, Cut-out in box.

2. Laboratory scene
A busy looking display can be created by placing dry ice in warm water in a flask connected to a system of tubes and containers. a, Carbon dioxide gas travels along the
tube. b, Glass tubes. c, Warm water. d, Coloured liquid. e, Dry ice.

Ray Guns and Blasters

These modern sci-fi weapons apparently demand more visual effect than hand guns and rifles. This applies even more to the unfortunate target, which must explode or disintegrate in a most dramatic fashion.

Weapons

Blasters and ray-guns come in all shapes and sizes, their design being limited only by such production needs as having to be carried or worn in holsters.

Smoke units attached to these props provide more credible results than flash bulbs or electric lights. Flash bulbs are too transitory to make an impact and internal lighting has to compete with the ambient light already set up in the studio. It is no good flicking a bulb on and off if the sleek contours of the weapon are already reflecting much more powerful studio lights.

Ray effects

These are often best achieved by overlaying a flashing light or an actual ray from another source. This is somewhat limiting because the shot must be carefully set up with the gun or the target fixed in relation to the rest of the scene. Only then can a shaft of light or a ripple effect be super-imposed over the main picture.

One effective method is to cut out a slot in a sheet of black paper and back it with opalescent glass or plastic. A tray of flash powder fired behind the slot gives a brilliant scorching effect emanating from the muzzle of the blaster.

If flash powder cannot be used, a light can be swept across the superimposed cut-out.

Target

Most ray-gun effects look good if the target erupts in a very conventional explosion. Methods of providing these are given on pages 88, 90, 96.

A further method of achieving a blast effect is to produce the blasted area in advance and then cover it with a removable membrane. For example, a cupboard door that has to be seared by the fearsome blast can be made of wood and the area required to be blasted hacked out with a chisel. Painted black and grey, a suitably devastated effect is implied. The treated door is then covered with self-adhesive wood-grain plastic sheet to make it look new.

To explode the area, a measure of gunpowder is applied to the sticky backing of the wood grain sheet before application, and a pyrofuse inserted through the back of the door to ignite it. The resultant explosion burns the sheet and blows it outward in a satisfactory searing effect.

RAY GUNS AND BLASTERS

For a superimposed ray effect, a fifty/fifty mirror can be used to combine the ray effect with the main scene. The ray, a slot cut in a black card, is illuminated by a flash-puff fired behind it.

For a blast effect a thin skin can be fastened over a prepared 'blasted' area. A very small charge is then sufficient to destroy the skin.

The Smoke Gun

Smoke that can be turned on and off when needed is an essential requirement in the making of films and television. Usually it is achieved by the use of a portable smoke machine, or hand held smoke gun. The two main types in present use are similar in principle, but one is electrically heated and the other is gas heated.

Electrically-heated gun

The method involved is that of heating mineral oil to a point where it turns into smoke. The temperature at which this happens is very critical. If it is too low the gun sprays hot oil; if it is too high the oil ignites and the gun becomes a flame-thrower.

Designs vary, but in general smoke is generated by passing the oil along a coiled tube or duct surrounding the heating element. This is done by introducing compressed gas or air into the sealed reservoir containing the oil. The oil is then driven by the pressure into the hot coil and converted into smoke.

The heating element in an electric gun is, of course, thermostatically controlled and, in order to maintain an even temperature, it is usual to embed the element in a steel block which acts as a heat store. This allows the gun to be used for some time after it has been disconnected from the supply; a useful feature where a long connecting lead would be an embarrassment.

Gas-heated gun

Although similar in principle to the electric gun, the gas gun has its coil heated by a butane or propane burner. This type of gun has to be ignited by a match or spark and usually should be extinguished when not in use to prevent damage to the coil.

Some guns have a hand-pumped air cylinder to pressurise the oil whilst others use the gas that also fuels the burner.

Using the smoke gun

The fact that studio guns are portable means that smoke can be introduced anywhere on the set and, being pressurised, can be directed where required. Flat funnels and pipe attachments can be used to direct smoke under doors and through small crevices.

Smoke, condensing on the cold walls of long lengths of pipe, reverts to oil which trickles downward. Oil traps (a simple closed tin with entrance and exit at the top will suffice) should be inserted at the lowest parts of the run to deal with this problem.

Smoke guns should never be pointed directly at actors nor discharged into flames.

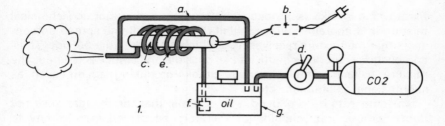

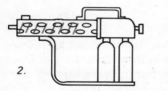

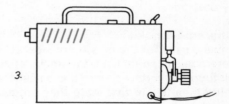

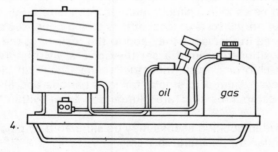

SMOKE GUN

Although smoke guns differ in size and have differing pressurisation and heating systems they nearly all work on a similar principle. Oil, pressurised in its container, is forced around a heated, coiled tube where it turns into smoke.

1. Principle of smoke gun
A small amount of carbon dioxide gas is fed to the oulet nozzle to reduce the risk of the heated oil igniting. a, By-pass. b, Switch, thermostat, fuse, indicator, light etc. c, Heater. d, Tap. e, Coil. f, Filter. g, Pressure tank.

2. Gas-heated hand held gun
Gas-heated guns are not generally suitable for studio use.

3. Studio gun electrically heated

4. Large outdoor gun, gas heated

Pyrotechnic and other Smokes

Pyrotechnic smoke is produced by igniting a slow-burning chemical mixture in a container which inhibits the rate of flame spread and ensures that the mixture receives no additional oxygen from outside. Thus, combustion is made as inefficient as possible and smoke is created. The mixture usually contains various smoke-producing agents such as naphthalene or bitumen, etc.

For smoke to be produced it is essential that the mixture does not flame. Smoke pots should not therefore be placed in proximity to anything that will catch fire, so igniting the smoke at the mouth of the pyrotechnic.

Charcoal smoke

Tablets used for the burning of incense in swinging censors for religious ceremonies can be used for smoke effects in the studio. Lit and placed on fireproof surfaces, or in tins on asbestos, they glow red-hot for about thirty minutes. In that state they produce no smoke, but if a few drops of machine oil are applied to the central unlit portion of charcoal a considerable amount of grey smoke is produced. This effect will last, diminishing gradually, until all the oil is used up. Barbecue charcoal briquettes can be used in a similar manner. Tablets or briquettes of this type are useful for all sorts of local effects which need to work without attention. Placed in fireplaces they add to the realism of the studio gas fires, while positioned around a set they give a vivid impression of a smokey night-club or a busy, industrial scene. They can be placed in studio chimneys required to smoke for long periods and also serve to authenticate camp fires that are illuminated from within by electric lights.

Burning food in cooking scenes may be simulated by placing a charcoal tablet under the incinerated items.

Hot-wire smoke

Occasionally it is required to produce an instant smoke effect where it is impractical to run a pipe from a smoke gun or to employ pyrotechnics. An answer to this situation is to use a short piece of nickel-chrome wire (the sort used in electric fire elements) which becomes red-hot when supplied with low-voltage current from a transformer or car battery. The wire should be wrapped around woven asbestos cloth or string impregnated with machine oil. When switched on the hot wire quickly causes the oil to smoke (although if too hot the oil will burst into flames). This technique has many applications, among which are smoking trousers and 'electrical equipment' which has to be seen to have some sort of dramatic short circuit or electric malfunction.

PYROTECHNIC AND OTHER SMOKES

1. A burning compressed-charcoal tablet gives off smoke when a few drops of oil are applied.
2. Principle of the heated steel wire encased in oil-impregnated asbestos tape.
3. A charcoal tablet being used to imply that food is burning.
4. The hot wire being used to simulate an overheated cable.
5. Some pyrotechnic smoke-pots are electrically fired, others have ignitable fuses.
6. Pyrotechnic smoke pots being used for location fire effect.

Flames

It is easy to set fire to any combustible material but the type of flame produced is not always permissible in film and TV studios.

Flaming brands

These should be made of an incombustible material (fireproofed wood is permissible) to which has been attached woven asbestos or asbestos string. The business end should be soaked in kerosene and allowed to stand upside down until *all* free liquid has drained off. Metal handles should not be used because they transmit heat.

Flame forks

Made from metal tubes these can be constructed in fan shapes or as tubes with drilled holes. Coupled by industrial-rubber hoses to a bottled-gas supply they are used to provide controllable flame wherever required. To obviate the risk of flash-over it is wise to have each flame fork ignited by an operator only as it is turned on. If this is not practical, it is feasible to have smaller pilot jets independently fed and positioned below the main flame forks.

Imitation flame

Red and yellow ribbons or torn silk strips fastened at their lower ends and blown upward in an air current can, when lit from below, look remarkably like flames. This is not an effect which is entirely realistic, but serves well enough where stylisation is acceptable.

Flame drum

A drum of transparent plastic, motorised to turn around slowly on a vertical axis, can be used for many lighting effects, but one of its most successful uses is that of illuminating a scene where the effect of flickering flames is required. The effect is achieved by painting the drum with sloping bands of black paint or sticking pieces of black paper to the outer surface. A powerful lamp shone through the rotating drum produces a flicerking light effect which travels upward as the paths of the black lines cross and re-cross each other.

A simpler version may be constructed from thick black paper into which has been cut a number of sloping ragged slots. If the paper is joined at its ends, forming it into a drum it can be fixed to a wooden cross and hung on a line. It can be wound up and then allowed to slowly unwind in front of a lamp.

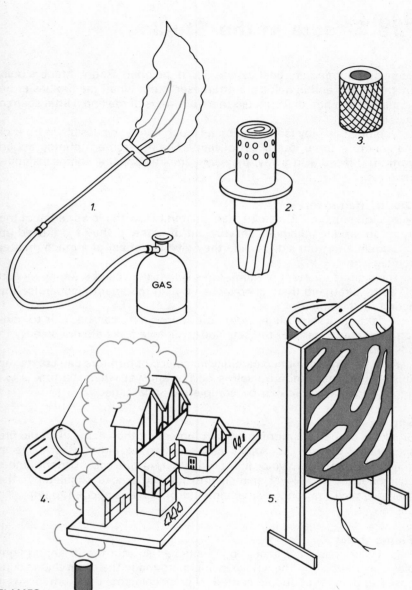

FLAMES

Practical flames can be introduced anywhere in the set if flame-forks (1) are used. Their effects can be heightened by using the flame-drum (5), a rotating cylinder of clear plastic on which is painted sloping shadows. A lamp shone through the drum produces cross-modulation of the clear patches, giving the effect of flames wreathing upward. For hand-held torches (2), impregnated asbestos tape may be packed into a short length of metal tube. An alternative head (3) comprises a thick stump of candle set inside a cylindrical lamp-wick. Back lit smoke (4) can seem to be a fierce conflagration when used with models.

Fire Effects in the Studio

Scenes of burning are best carried out in the open. Room interiors built on studio lots and in fields are often used — but when the fire has to be simulated in a film or TV studio there are ways of making a little seem a lot.

One obvious ploy is to position as much flame as possible in front of the action. A three foot sheet of flame fills the frame if photographed from 7ft. Placed 30ft away, the same amount of flame seems insignificant.

Use of flame forks

Flame forks (page 74) can be manipulated below the lower edge of the frame to produce a significant amount of flame. If they are moved up and down and from side to side they give the effect of a much greater conflagration.

The significant asset of flame-forks is that they can be turned on and off as required and there is no loose burning material to jeopardise the action in the studio.

If flame-forks are made from soft copper they can be bent to conform to various parts of the set. Non-malleable forks are not so easy to position.

A flame fork positioned carefully in a piece of furniture can create the illusion that the furniture itself is on fire and yet when the fork is extinguished the article can be completely undamaged.

Smoke

Smoke is probably a more important ingredient than flame in studio fire sequences. Cleverly lit, smoke can seem to be almost flame-like in quality without involving the production in fire risk. Bright lights positioned at floor level shining into moving smoke supplement the scene so well that only a small amount of flame is needed to imply an inferno.

Flame drum

This device (page 74) should be positioned so that the flickering light plays on walls or on the smoke swirling around in the room that is supposed to be on fire. Supplemented by practical flame the drum makes it appear that the bulk of the fire is to one side of the picture. It is often more dramatic to imply that the body of the fire is outside the frame of the picture and that the viewer is seeing only the reflected glow.

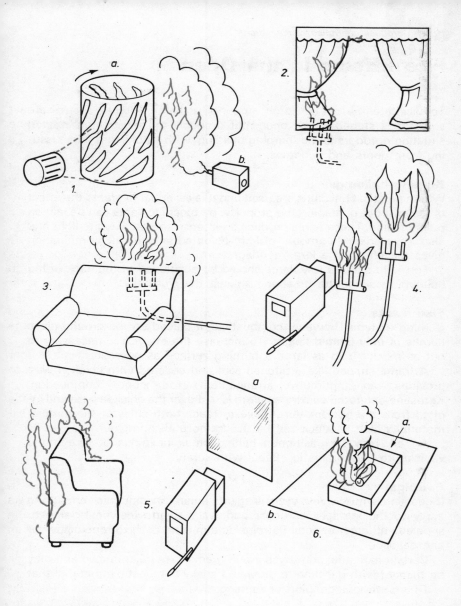

FIRE EFFECTS IN THE STUDIO

1. Smoke lit from a lamp shining through a flame drum. a, Flame drum. b, Smoke machine.
2. Indestructible glass fibre curtains used with flame fork.
3. Flame fork behind furniture.
4. Flame forks in front of camera.
5. Flaming 'furniture shaped' rig being superimposed over real furniture, using fifty/fifty mirror technique. a, Semi-transparent mirror.
6. Pyrotechnic flare being burnt to provide both light and smoke. a, Sand tray. b, Fireproof sheet.

Fire Effects in the Open

To facilitate the use of large amounts of flame, interior scenes are sometimes staged in the open, but probably the most often created situation outdoors is the 'burning building' with smoke and flame issuing from doors and windows.

Burning buildings

Where practical buildings are used and it is essential to create the effect of fire without damaging the property, pyrotechnic flares can be laid on trays of sand. These flares produce an intense source of white light and also a considerable amount of light-coloured smoke. The combination gives the effect of a large conflagration.

For night shots a few flares should be positioned at the back of the building to silhouette its shape against the night sky.

Flame arks

Burning material, however combustible, if placed on the ground gives' flames of only limited height. To increase the effect it is necessary to get as much air to as large a burning surface as possible.

A frame shaped like a pitched roof and covered with chicken wire provides an optimum arrangement for good combustion. Kerosene-saturated sacking or cloth is laid over the chicken wire and ignited from the bottom. Air is able to reach both sides of the burning material which is supported by the frame until burnt out.

An ark may be positioned behind small buildings or foreground vehicles to give dramatic effects with safety.

Petrolgel

If gasoline is mixed with various agents it can be made thick enough to apply to the surfaces of doors and walls to provide local flame to supplement larger effects. Petrolgel is a mixture of thixotrophic powder and gasoline.

Certain industrial adhesives are in themselves inflammable and may be thinned with gasoline to provide a sticky combustible material that will burn without dripping or running.

WARNING: Be sensible!

Place fire extinguishers and buckets of water close to the sources of fire effects.

Make sure that all personnel involved have free access to safety before igniting effects.

Remember that a building full of smoke can endanger the lives of people in areas not directly involved in the fire sequence.

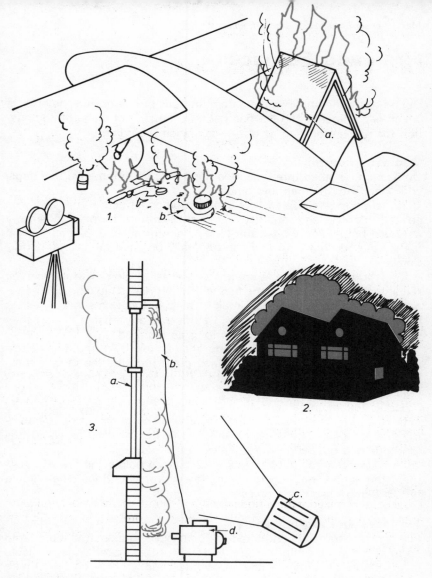

FIRE EFFECTS IN THE OPEN

1. Wreckage
A burning aircraft can be simulated by using large flames behind with small pieces of burning wreckage scattered in the foreground. a, Flame ark. b, Burning pieces in foreground.

2. Burning buildings
Back-lit smoke at the rear of a building gives a good effect at night.

3. Burning rooms
Burning rooms can be suggested by using smoke and light. a, Half-open window. b, Polythene sheet. c, Lamp. d, Smoke gun.

Fires and Furnaces

Open fires in the studio can create numerous problems, not the least of which is continuity. The fire has to be at the correct stage of combustion for retakes on film or out-of-sequence recording.

Domestic hearth

Domestic fires need three main components: imitation solid fuel (logs, coal, peat etc.), flames and smoke.

Imitation logs and pieces of coal can be constructed from asbestos soaked in water and moulded round chicken-wire formers. When dry they can be painted with water-based paint or dyes. Subjected to real flames they do not burn and can generally be used for several performances.

Gas burners situated among the pieces of dummy fuel can be regulated to provide authentic flames. The burners should be open-ended pipes with no separate air intake. The gas then burns with a yellow flame and not an unnatural blue. Gas flames are reliable in that they will burn without variation for as long as required.

Some types of domestic firelighter may be used. To create flame this material can be cut or broken up and placed around the dummy fuel. Usually these firelighters emit quite a lot of smoke, which adds to the realism.

Liquid fuel in containers should be avoided, but asbestos tape wired in bundle form can be soaked in kerosene and burnt alongside the dummy coal or logs. Care must be taken with this method as liquid fuel tends to drip out when the bundles are burning.

Smoking charcoal tablets (page 72) placed below the fire will augment the flames, but should be kept away from the drips where liquid fuel is being used on bundles.

Furnaces and red-hot coals

For braziers, furnaces and stove, it is possible to use an electric lamp surrounded by glass fibre. Some varieties of this material are available in a suitable pink/orange hue, but white varieties may be tinted with spirit-based dyes. Alternatively, the light source may be coloured.

Dobs of black and grey paint applied to the outside layers of the glass-fibre add realism. Flames are not usually required for this type of fire, but smoke can be used as above.

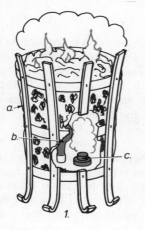

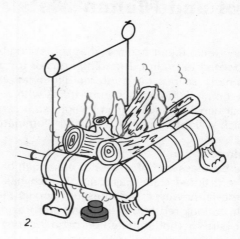

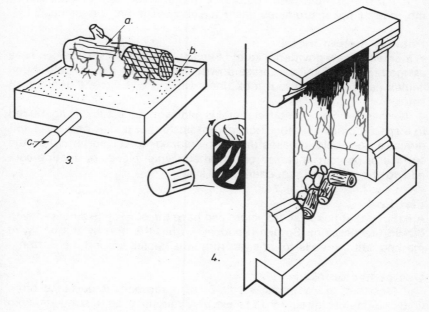

FIRES AND FURNACES

1. A brazier constructed of glass fibre with internal lighting and a charcoal smoke unit.
a, Glass fibre. b, Lamp. c, Charcoal tablet.
2. Log fire using piped gas and charcoal tablet.
3. Indestructible log with flames fed by gas dispersed in a sand tray. a, Log made from
asbestos-covered chicken wire. b, Sand. c, Gas.
4. Augmented fire effect using flame drum to supply illumination.

Hot and Molten Metal

It is often difficult to show that something being used in a production is supposed to be hot. Branding irons or torture implements used in dark dramatic scenes need internal illumination. To seem convincing they must emit light and illuminate items with which they come into contact. Clear acrylic plastic transmits light so it can be used to make articles in which a light source at one end illuminates the other.

Pokers
The business end of a red-hot poker can be mocked up by constructing it from tinted clear plastic into which has been inserted a small bulb. There is, however, a fluorescent acrylic plastic that needs no internal light to look red-hot. If the ends are provided with smoke by using the hot-wire method outlined on page 72 they appear suitably convincing.

A felt-pad treated with liquid make-up and secreted at the back of the red-hot poker produces nasty looking burns on human flesh.

Pouring molten metal
Water with finely powdered aluminium sprinkled on its surface can pass as molten lead. Similarly, brass powder appears as molten gold. Such liquids can be poured, but look unconvincing without the addition of smoke.

A realistic effect of molten metal is achieved if the liquid is contained in a special crucible with a transparent bottom of plastic or glass. Light directed from below makes the 'metal' appear to be red-hot when the surface of powder is stirred or disturbed. Small pieces of floating cork add to the realism by appearing as slag.

Flat iron
A flat iron that has to scorch cloth can have the sole-plate smeared with brown grease-paint. Smoke produced within the iron by the hot wire method can be made to emerge from small holes around the bottom.

Use of heated items
The fact that safety in the studio is of paramount importance often leads effects designers to go to extraordinary lengths to simulate even the most mundane activity. Red-hot metal being quenched in water is a typical example. In such cases it is wise to consider using the real thing. The alternative is to screen something which looks less than realistic and is much more expensive.

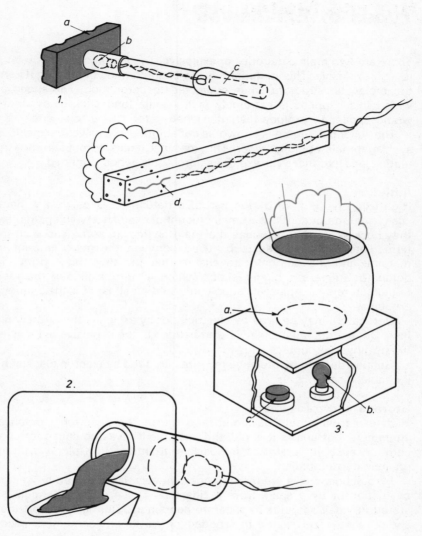

HOT AND MOLTEN METAL

1. Branding irons
Red-hot pokers, branding irons, etc. must emit light and sometimes smoke. a, Fluorescent plastic. b, Lamp. c, Battery. d, Hot wire smoke.

2. Pouring molten metal
Water poured from a pot with a transparent bottom and built-in lamp. Even when poured the water continues to transmit the light.

3. Simulated hot metal
The metal itself is never seen, but the light and the smoke arising imply that hot metal is contained within. a, Open base. b, Lamp. c, Charcoal tablet.

Types of Explosives

There are two main categories of explosive. The first and most powerful is high explosive. This material has the characteristic of altering its entire molecular structure when subjected to detonation. The speed at which this happens is extremely fast. A mile long stick of dynamite would appear to explode instantly when detonated at one end.

The second category is known as deflagrating explosive and includes such materials as gunpowder. This material needs combustion for initiation and produces its explosive force only when confined.

Initiation

High explosive is fired by the use of a detonator. Usually in a metal case, a detonator contains a small amount of explosive which generates the shock wave that explodes the main charge. In some cases an intermediate explosive has to be used between the main amount of material and the detonator to ensure that the tiny shock from the detonator triggers a bigger shock which in turn explodes the rest. Manufacturers of explosives supply information sheets for their various products.

Detonators may be fired by electricity or by an ignitable pyrotechnic fuse. Detonators must always be embedded in the explosive or be in intimate physical contact with it.

Gunpowder and pyrotechnic mixtures are fired by electric fuses or by ignitable fuses.

Storage and transport

High explosive should be stored and transported in strong, practical containers, but unless it is old and unstable it gives no cause for concern because it is almost impossible to make it explode without preliminary detonation.

Pyrotechnic mixes are more dangerous because they can be ignited by friction or by a spark from a cigarette. These mixtures should be stored in small amounts in separate containers. During transport they should always be sealed in wooden or cardboard containers inside metal boxes.

Uses

It is impossible to lay down absolute guide lines for the use of explosives, but generally it should be remembered that deflagrating explosions are slow while detonating explosions are fast. This very much dictates the uses to which they are put. For example, if something is to be blown into the air (say a block of wood out of a steel mortar) gunpowder should be used. High explosive would reduce the wood to fragments.

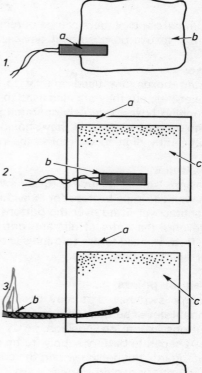

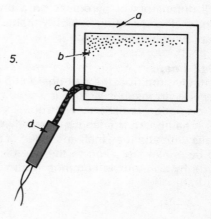

Methods of igniting or detonating the two types of explosives.
1. a, Detonator. b, High explosive.
2. a, Strong case. b, Pyrofuse. c, Gunpowder.
3. a, Strong case. b, Fuse. c, Gunpowder.
4. a, Detonator. b, High explosive. c, Fuse.
5. a, Strong case. b, Gunpowder. c, Fuse. d, Pyrofuse.

Firing Boxes and Exploders

Commercial exploders can be purchased, but for effects work it is often better to use purpose-built devices.

Uses
Firing boxes are used mainly to fire pyrotechnics, explosives and bullet-hits, but they are also used to operate such things as panel lights, dropping boxes, remotely operated props and many other things. Used with long runs of cable they should be capable of supplying a voltage sufficiently high to overcome the resistance of the wire.

Facilities
Designs should include a rotary switch for rapid-sequence operations as well as single buttons for individual items. A permanent, transparent, plastic cover fitted over the buttons allows them to be used freely, but prevents the entry of dirt and grit.

Robust, easy to use terminals should be incorporated and situated as far apart as practicable.

Danger points
Toggle switches that may be inadvertently left in the 'on' position should *never* be used, but remember that grit and sand can jam push buttons in the 'on' position.

A separate battery supply, to be connected only at the last moment, safeguards the person wiring the charges. To make absolutely sure that it is not connected, *he* can carry it with him.

Indicator lamp circuits should be carefully designed so that they do not provide a secondary path to the terminals.

Circuits
If a firing box operates on a low-voltage high current, it is advisable to fire detonators or pyrofuses on a parallel circuit. If a commercial exploder, incorporating a high-voltage magneto, is used then the items may be wired in series.

Nail board
Entirely primitive, the nail-board still turns up from time to time. It has several virtues; it is simple, the circuit can be plainly seen and the speed of operation is easy to control.

A nail-board is a length of wood into which has been driven a row of nails with about an inch and a half of nail left protruding. Wires soldered to each nail are taken to the pyrotechnics or bullet hits and these are fired by wiping the common return lead along the row of nails.

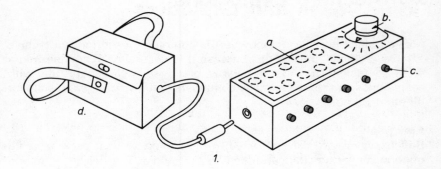

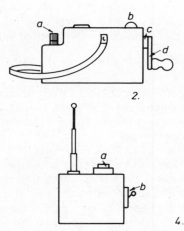

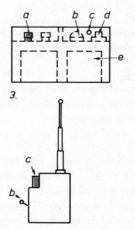

FIRING BOXES AND EXPLODERS

1. General purpose firing box

The battery supply is detachable and can be carried by the person wiring up the charges. Not suitable for very long cable runs. a, Press buttons behind plastic shield. b, Rotary switch. c, Terminals. d, Battery case.

2. High-voltage magneto type

Fires one circuit only, but suitable for long distance work with a large number of charges wired in series. a, Terminals. b, Pilot light. c, Press button. d, Handle.

3. Simple battery box

A basic type with on/off switch, red indicator light and single press-button to fire one circuit. Ideal for studio work. a, Terminals. b, Pilot light. c, Switch. d, Press button. e, Batteries.

4. Radio controlled unit

Receiver capable of firing one local circuit only. Because this can be situated where a human operator would be at risk it is suitable for low-voltage, short distance cable runs. a, Press button. b, Switch. c, Terminals.

Pyrotechnic Explosions

Mealed black powder (gunpowder) is commonly used for pyrotechnic explosive effects, but for this purpose it is necessary to confine it in a stout container. The most popular is, of course, a cardboard tube with sealed ends, but there are many containers that give different results for different purposes.

Flat pack
Stiff paper or card can be folded to make a convenient pack for firing gunpowder for small local effects in the studio. The design permits a pyrofuse to be used without the necessity for special sealing. A few turns of adhesive tape around the pack secures both powder and fuse. If the pack is tightly wrapped in tape it has a greater explosive effect.

The flat-pack can conveniently be placed under wax bottles or vases, or between rows of books.

Maroons
A maroon (firework bomb) is usually a stout cardboard case holding a quantity of black powder. The larger ones have their ends sealed with discs of wood and are wrapped with many turns of string before being dipped in a hardening and sealing compound.

Maroons are useful for simulating bombs or shell fire. Put at the bottom of pre-dug holes in the ground they can be covered with dry peat and broken cork pieces and fired remotely. If actors or stunt men are to run close to the maroon the firing can be achieved by the use of a trip wire. Two spring-loaded contacts are kept apart by a piece of insulating material which, being attached to the wire, is pulled free when the actor runs into it.

Mortar
A stout iron tube with one end sealed to a base plate may be used to project things into the air. A bag of gunpowder is placed at the bottom of the tube after which paper is pushed in to form a 'wad'. On top of this is placed a wooden dowel, the diameter of which is an easy fit in the mortar. Dummy men, oil-drums, trees, wooden sheds may all be 'blown up' in this fashion. Flash-pots or gunpowder packs positioned at ground level supplement the explosion by providing a visual flash.

Large explosions
An oil drum sunk into the ground and filled with a mixture of gasoline and bitumen can be fired by placing several maroons in the bottom of the can. They should be well sealed in plastic bags and weighted so that they sink to the bottom. The resultant fire-ball filmed in slow motion resembles a nuclear holocaust.

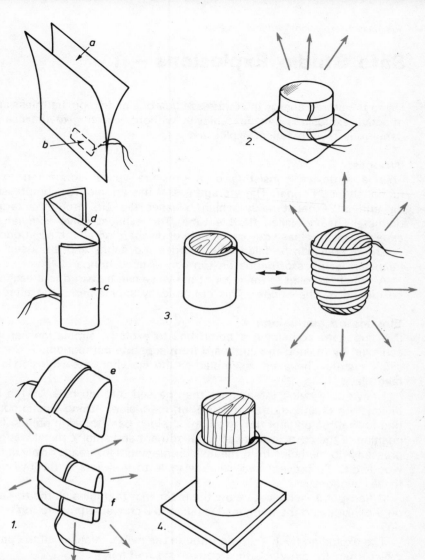

PYROTECHNIC EXPLOSIONS

1. Flat pack
Used for mild flashes and bangs in the studio. a, First paper fold. b, Pyrofuse. c, Second and third folds. d, Filling. e, Fourth fold. f, Adhesive tape.

2. Flash puff
Used for studio flash and smoke effects. The top is thin paper.

3. Ground maroon
Used for general explosive effects. It consists of a cardboard case with wooden ends and is wound round with string.

4. Steel mortar
A stout iron tube anchored to a base plate. A gunpowder charge propels the wooden block upward with considerable force.

89

Safe Studio Explosions — 1

Using the stored energy in compressed air or elastic rope, harmless and effective explosions can be achieved without resorting to the use of dangerous or impractical explosives.

Whoofer

This is a device consisting of a pressure vessel connected to a funnel-shaped hopper. The storage vessel has an inlet for compressed air and an exhaust valve which releases the air through a large-diameter, heavy-walled flexible tube. The exhaust valve is a large-capacity quick-release device capable of discharging all the air at once.

The hopper can be filled with powder and debris and it is usual to heap further piles of debris on top of the filled hopper.

A switch coupled to the lever of the valve can be wired to a flashpot positioned by the hopper. This dramatically supplements the effect.

Elasticated explosions

If a cupboard containing a bomb has to explode, simulation can be achieved by making the cupboard from separate components — doors, sides, top etc. These are assembled on the set where the explosion is to take place.

Heavy-duty nylon threads are then passed through holes in the individual parts and knotted together on the inside. Strong elastic cords tied to the free ends of the nylon are strained back to fixing points. The position of the parts is checked for alignment and small conical wedges pressed into the holes from the inside, trapping the threads firmly in the woodwork. To prevent slip it is advisable to tie knots in the nylon at these junctions.

A flashpot is hung just below the main knot that joins all the threads on the inside and the firing lead is taken to a convenient operating position.

The exploding flash, burning through the nylon, releases all the parts which then fly outwards in a convincing manner.

To enhance the effect from such dummy explosions the nylon threads may be fastened to inanimate objects around the site of the bomb. For example, a suitcase or parcel bomb can be made to release threads which pull chairs, lamps, carpets etc. from around the blasted area.

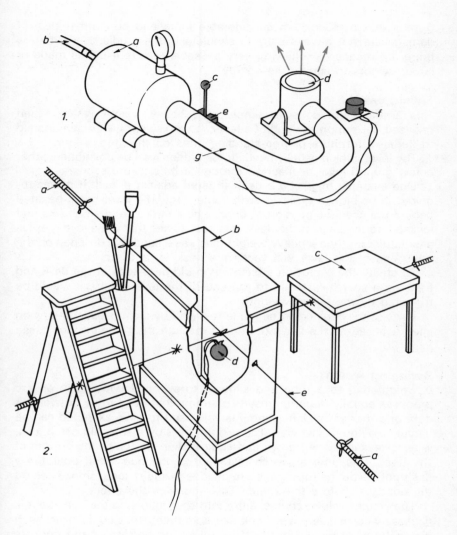

SAFE STUDIO EXPLOSIONS

1. The 'whoofer'
a, Compressed air vessel. b, Input. c, Exhaust valve. d, Discharge pot. e, Switch. f, Flash puff. g, Flexible pipe.

2. Elasticated explosion
a, Elastic. b, Crate in separate parts. c, Lightweight table. d, Flash bomb. e, Nylon cord.

Safe Studio Explosions — 2

Bombs that explode with considerable force and do a great deal of damage are not always easy to simulate in the studio. Nevertheless there are means of achieving very passable results if use is made of large weights to supply the energy.

Falling weight

This arrangement consists simply of a heavy weight which, when released, falls upon the end of a lever. It works very well when applied to items of furniture or free-standing units on the studio floor.

The lever, which usually needs to be hidden, can be positioned either below ground level or inserted through a hole in the scenery.

One example might be a desk situated against a wall. If it was required to be blown to pieces with some force, the lever could be sited behind the scenery, passing through a hole in the set wall and its end locked into the back of the desk. It is easy to see that if the lever passes over a fulcrum then a heavy weight (such as a sandbag) dropped on the other end of the lever will cause the desk to jump up.

To create the explosion a flash-pot could be placed in the desk and fired via a switch fastened to the end of the lever where it would be triggered by the falling weight.

Parts of the desk could be made to fly off by using elastic and nylon lines released as the flashpot burned through the tethering point (see page 90)

Swinging weight

A weight tied to a rope and allowed to swing downward in an arc produces equally dramatic results on items that need to fly outward. A door of a room in which a bomb is supposed to have exploded can be fiercely ejected in this way. The weight, held by a solenoid catch, can, when released, sweep down and strike either the top or the bottom of the door. This time a switch fastened on the door itself operates a flash-pot inside the room. It is a good idea to squirt some smoke behind the door just before the action. This improves the effect.

The weight will, of course, enter into shot following the door, so it is necessary to disguise it to look like something that could have been blown from inside the room. If it strikes the bottom of the door its progress can be halted by fixing a second line tied to a dragging sandbag anchor. If it is at the top it can be released from its rope by having a nylon loop which is destroyed by a detonator fired simultaneously with the studio flash.

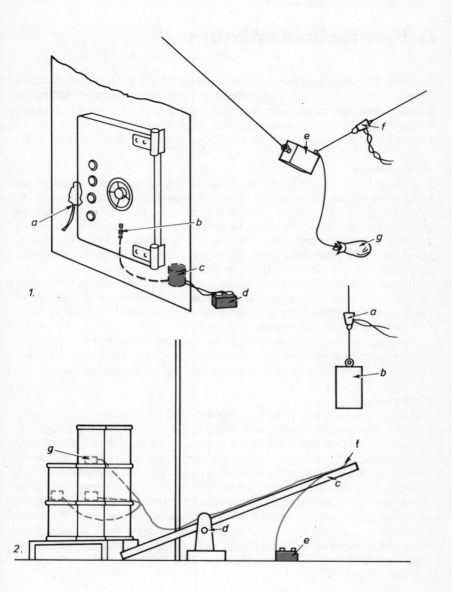

SAFE STUDIO EXPLOSIONS

1. Swinging weight
a, Mock fuse and explosive. b, Switch. c, Flash pot. d, Battery. e, Weight. f, 'Bomb'
release. g, Sandbag drag anchor.

2. Falling weight
a, 'Bomb' release. b, Weight. c, Lever. d, Fulcrum. e, Battery. f, Switch. g, Flatpacks.

A Pyrotechnic Mixture

In many countries pyrotechnic manufacture is subject to regulation and may be carried out only by registered workers in an approved factory or building. In some cases even the simple cutting of a firework is deemed to be 'manufacturing'. Nevertheless, permission may usually be obtained by effects personnel to carry out essential work in this field.

Basic recipe

The most widely used material is composed of the three substances, potassium nitrate, sulphur and charcoal. Mixed in the proportions 75%, 10% and 15% respectively, it is a fast burning material which can be classified as gunpowder, albeit of a crude type. Its explosive qualities depend on many things; the fineness of the powders, the uniform distribution of the components throughout the mix and so on. Its efficiency also depends on the conditions at the time of ignition.

Packed tightly into a sealed container it will almost certainly explode as the rapid rise of pressure and temperature causes acceleration of combustion to explosion point. Conversely, spread out on a flat surface, the same mixture will merely burn rapidly.

Varying the proportions allows the mixture to burn more slowly.

It is simpler and more convenient to use commercial mealed black powder for fireworks requiring rapid burning or explosion.

Flashpowder

Generally it is better to purchase flashpowder as a ready-made material as there are certain dangers in making it. Some mixtures have high explosive properties and have been known to cause serious accidents.

A reasonable substitute can be achieved by mixing flaked or powdered aluminium or magnesium with mealed gunpowder. The proportions should be experimented with as too bright a flash can often prove to be unacceptable for television cameras. Mixtures should, where possible, be produced freshly when required, because the metal powders in contact with the chemicals tend to oxidise, affecting the resultant burning of the mix. Of the two metals, aluminium is probably more stable as the oxide that forms tends to protect the metal from further action.

Use

These mixtures may be used for creating explosions, flash and smoke effects, gunpowder trails and so on. They may be fired in mortars and pans and may be made up into maroons, fuses and simulated rockets.

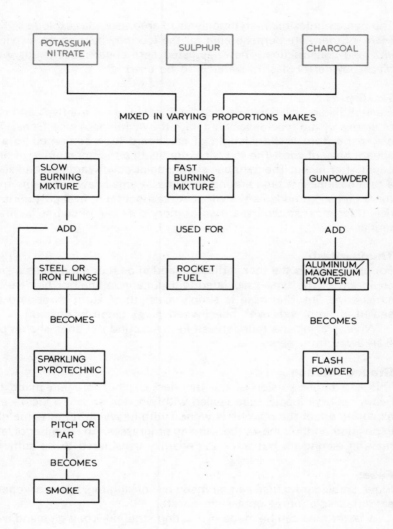

PYROTECHNIC MIXTURE

Most pyrotechnic materials used in effects work consist of mixtures of the three basic constituents — potassium nitrate, sulphur and charcoal. Explosive or burning characteristics depend on the quality of the raw materials, the mix and the packing.

95

Pyrotechnic Construction

The pyrotechnics most commonly used are those that explode or flash. Many of them are purpose built for the job they have to do, varying in size and construction. The ones listed here cover most needs where black powder or flash powder is to be used.

Flash puff
Flash puffs are invariably used at floor level to create a flash and cloud of smoke of the type associated with the appearance of a Genie. They are made from a short length of cardboard tube cemented to a flat square base of card. The top is covered with a thin membrane of tissue paper after filling. The pyrofuse should point downward and be fixed by a turn of adhesive tape around the tube. A small saw cut in the top of the tube accommodates the wires. A teaspoonful of flashpowder is sufficient for most studio uses. Two or more pots can of course be fired in tandem.

Thunderflash
For use outdoors the thunderflash buried in peat or sand gives a small explosion of the type associated with a cannon shell or high-velocity small-arms fire. The case is simply a length of stout cardboard tube sealed at both ends with beechwood plugs glued in position.
   When placing the thunderflash in the ground the ends should point well away from personnel.

Ground maroon
This is a larger version of the thunderflash, but is again made from heavy-wall cardboard tube sealed with wooden ends. To increase the explosive effect the maroon is wound with heavy string or twine glued in position on the tube as the winding progresses. Any number of layers may be wound on but three is generally considered to be sufficient.

Fuses
Slow, smouldering fuse can be made by soaking rag, paper or rope in a saturated solution of potassium nitrate.
   A faster fuse can be made by coating string in wood glue and, while the glue is still tacky, rolling the string in mealed gunpowder.
   For an even faster fuse (quickmatch) the above string fuse inserted into a paper sleeve will fire rapidly.
   The string (without the paper sleeve) may be slowed down by saturating it in a solution of methylated spirit and shellac.

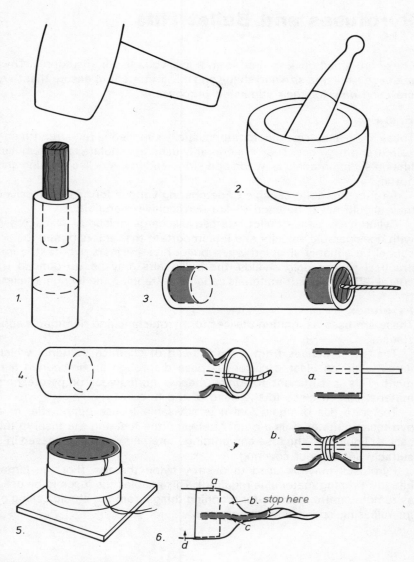

PYROTECHNIC CONSTRUCTION

1. Wooden implements are used for filling and tamping. Ends may be plugged with wood or clay.
2. Each ingredient is ground separately, mixing only small quantities at a time.
3. Explosive thunder flash made from cardboard tube with glued-in wooden ends.
4. Rocket case with constricted throat. a, Soak in water and insert mandrel. b, Bind with string. Remove the mandrel when dry.
5. Flash puff case with tissue paper top.
6. Method of applying touch paper fuse. a, Glue. b, Touch paper. c, Quick-match fuse. d, Case.

Pyrofuses and Bullet Hits

These are small devices fired from a low-voltage electric source. They are each similar in size and shape and it is important to ensure that they are used *only* for their stipulated purposes.

Bullet hits

These are plastic-cased detonators usually supplied in full-strength and half-strength grades. They are primarily used to simulate realistic bullet hits on such materials as wood and stone and in items like clothing and bottles.

As they are quite capable of detonating various forms of explosives they should never be used to fire pyrotechnic materials.

Cylindrically cased bullet hits can discharge pieces of plastic case with considerable velocity and it is important that actors or studio personnel be suitably shielded when bullet hits are fired. Where it is impractical to use rigid shields, the bullet hits may be surrounded by energy-absorbing soft materials capable of trapping the flying particles.

Pyrofuses

These are used as ignition devices for pyrotechnic and flammable substances.

The effect derives from a small bead of chemical material which flares when an electric current is passed through an embedded filament. This is sufficient to ignite mealed gunpowder or pyrotechnic material placed close to the head of the fuse.

To ignite gas or liquid fuel it is advisable to use gunpowder or a pyrotechnic material as a primer between the fuel and the fuse. In the case of liquid fuel the fuse and priming material should be encased in a suitably liquid-proof covering.

Pyrofuses may be used to destroy nylon threads. (For the larger gauges, priming material is required). This enables the fuses to be used as remote control devices for dropping things from the studio ceiling or for releasing spring devices in props.

PYROFUSES AND BULLET HITS

Pyrofuse.

Plastic cased detonator or bullet-hit.

Metal-cased detonator.

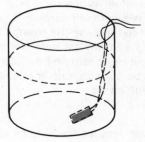

Pyrofuses should always be positioned where they will be in contact with
combustible material.

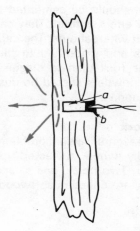

Bullet-hit embedded in wood just
under the surface. a, Bullet-hit. b,
Wood or clay plug.

Flying splinters and spurting dust.

Bullet Effects in Scenery

Walls and stonework in the studio are of different materials, and pose different problems, from those used on location.

Walls
The walls in the studio are scenic flats surfaced with artificial brickwork, plaster or wallpaper and are not thick enough to permit realistic effects. The areas in which bullet holes are to appear are therefore backed with blocks of wood in which the holes can be sculpted in advance and then filled with powder and chips and covered with fresh surfacing material. The holes can subsequently be blasted out with plastic bullet hits or pyrofuses fitted with capsules of black powder. An alternative method is to fix steel tubes to the backs of flats.

The type of wall surface is very important. Large plain areas make it difficult to disguise the treated spots whereas unduly busy or patterned surfaces can almost hide the final bullet holes. On location, if an outdoor wall must remain free from damage, it can have false work modelled on the surface with modelling clay. A small pocket of dust provides sufficient effect.

Rocks
Both real and artificial rocks can be treated similarly. First a prepared hole is made on the surface then the bullet hit is laid in the depression. The leads should be cemented to the surface if they are not to fly up when the effect is fired. They can be covered in modelling clay to disguise their whereabouts. The depression should be filled in with powder and chips and smoothed to the original contours. As it is easier to colour the rock than to disguise the prepared hole, suitably blended coloured powders should be dusted liberally all over the area until the holes disappear.

Woodwork
Wood presents fewer problems than other materials as it splits realistically when subjected to the explosive force of a bullet-hit detonator. Two holes, one to accommodate the detonator and one for the wires, are drilled in softwood and the hole is then plugged and disguised.

Direction
Bullet effects often appear far too contrived. To give maximum value for money they tend to run in a straight line up the middle of the frame. It is often easier and more effective to position them erratically in less exposed areas.

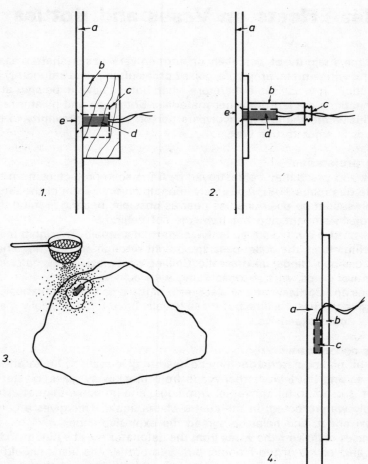

BULLET EFFECTS IN SCENERY

1. Holes in walls
Scenic flats are not thick enough for realistic effects, so the bullet hole area is usually backed with a wood block. a, Scenic flat. b, Wooden block. c, Powder. d, Half charge bullet hit. e, Prepared area surfaced with paper.

2. An alternative
A steel tube can be used instead of a wooden block. a, Scenic flat. b, Steel tube. c, Screw-in plug. d, Bullet hit. e, Prepared area surfaced with paper.

3. Bullet-struck rocks
A prepared hole takes the bullet hit which is covered with chips and powder.

4. Replacement panels
If, because of rehearsal requirements, the same areas have to be used several times a method must be chosen whereby the holes can be made good by re-papering or by the replacement of suitable panels. a, Replacement panel of timber or board. b, Metal plate. c, Bullet hit.

Bullet Effects on Vases and Bottles

While the majority of porcelain or earthenware vases shatter easily when hit with a metal projectile, glass bottles often prove stubbornly indestructible. It is advisable therefore when bottles have to be shot at to use imitations made from other materials. Both wax and plaster react well, but where the action involves a person in close proximity to the bottle, it is safer to use wax.

Using projectiles
Bottles and vases may be destroyed by firing solid projectiles from the capsule gun (page 108). Accurately lined up on the centre of the target the gun should be positioned as near as possible, bearing in mind that the projectile might ricochet from the set behind.

Wax bottles tend to soften in the warmth of a studio. This inhibits the shattering effect, the bullet passing straight through and leaving a hole that is disappointingly un-dramatic. Chilling on a block of dry ice or in a refrigerator helps, as also does filling with cold water.

Vases and bottles made of clear resin of the type used for breakaway glass give the best results, but these usually have to be specially made and are more expensive.

Using detonators
Bullet-hit plastic detonators may be used to give realistic bullet effects on vases and bottles whether made from breakaway glass, plaster or wax. It is usual to fill the vessel with liquid and immerse the detonator (suitably waterproofed) in the centre of the liquid. This gives a better pictorial effect, and helps to spread the explosive shock.

In vases of flowers the wires from the detonator may be hidden in the stalks and leaves of the blooms, but with bottles the leads should be taken through a small hole low down in the back.

A simpler method is to situate the detonators under the bottles, hidden in the table or shelf on which the items stand. Success depends on having liquid in the vessels to spread the shock.

Using the dropping weight
A vase may be broken without using either projectile or detonator if a cone shaped plug is inserted in the neck and a line (tied to the plug) is passed through a hole in the base. A suitably heavy weight tied to the other end of the line need only be dropped a few inches to demolish the vase.

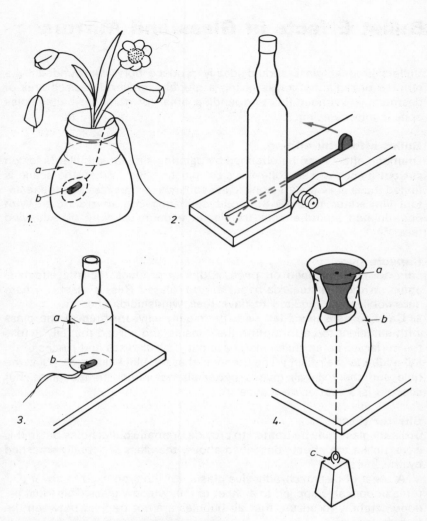

BULLET EFFECT ON VASES AND BOTTLES

1. Exploded from inside
a, Water. b, Waterproofed bullet hit. The water spreads the explosive effect.

2. Mechanical shattering
Where explosives cannot be used, a rapidly moving spring arm can be used as a projectile.

3. External detonator
a, Water. b, Bullet hit hidden in shelf.

4. Dropping weight
a, Conical plug. b, Wax vase. When the weight drops the plug is pulled into the vase and breaks its neck. The plug should be disguised to look like a piece of broken vase.

Bullet Effects in Glass and Mirrors

Bullets fired at glass should ideally produce holes surrounded by a number of radiating cracks giving a roughly circular, fist-sized area of destruction. Without this surrounding area of damage, bullet holes appear unconvincing.

Bullet effect by editing
Dramatic effects can be obtained by painting simulated bullet holes on cut-out pieces of self-adhesive clear plastic sheet. When the scene is filmed these cut-outs are applied in sequence to the glass and the resultant film edited to show the holes appearing one after another. With post-dubbed sound-effects this is an economical way of achieving results.

Capsule gun
This device (described on page 108) can produce realistic effects — again, without actual damage to the glass. This is useful where automobiles are required to have their windshields shot at.

Gelatine capsules filled with petroleum jelly are fired at the glass with sufficient force to rupture the capsule and spread the jelly across the surface. The capsules may have small black discs and pieces of tin foil added to their filling. The theory is that the black disc resembles the hole and the foil will give a better shatter effect on the glass, but success is a matter of chance.

Shatter glass
Ordinary glass may be treated to provide dramatic bullet holes but in this case, unlike the effects described above, the glass is actually smashed by the impact.

A sheet of clear, self-adhesive plastic (of the type used to cover pictures or books) is applied to a sheet of thin window glass. This must be done carefully to ensure that air bubbles are not trapped between the two materials.

Mirrors may be similarly treated, but the plastic sheet in this instance need not be clear.

To produce the bullet holes in glass treated in this fashion it is necessary to fire a projectile right through it. The capsule gun, this time loaded with steel slugs, produces an admirable effect.

A mirror can appear to be shattered by a bullet if a captive, spring-loaded bolt is released from behind. Few splinters of glass escape from the adhesive backing, but if an actor is close to the mirror, it should be fronted with a protective sheet of acrylic plastic.

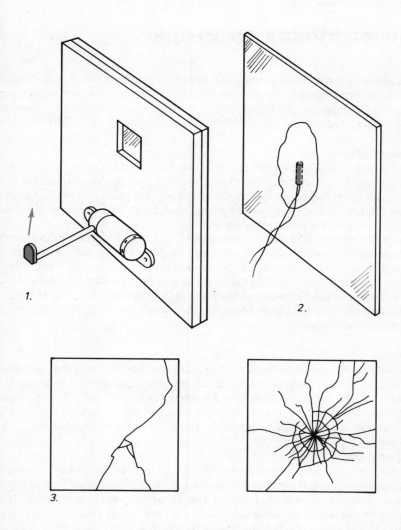

1.

2.

3.

BULLET EXPLOSIONS IN GLASS AND MIRRORS

1. Mechanical method
A spring-loaded door closer can be used to smash a mirror from behind.

2. Explosive method
A mirror can be shattered by placing a bullet-hit behind it and covering the spot with a chunk of modelling clay. This method must not be used close to actors as small fragments of glass are projected with considerable force.

3. Improving the effect
Mirrors or sheets of glass that are shot at with metal projectiles (including the spring arm) will break disappointingly (*left*) unless they are covered at the back with adhesive plastic sheet. This produces a much more satisfactory visual effect (*right*).

Bullet Effects on People

'Walking toward the window, the man is suddenly riddled with bullets —'. So might the studio directions appear in a script. But to achieve such human destruction the effects designer must employ protective devices to ensure that he does not injure the actor playing the part.

Bullet plates
These are metal plates designed to protect performers who are to be subjected to bullet hits. The plates worn under clothing, must be sufficiently thick to absorb the shock of the explosion and formed in such a way that no part of the person's body can be in line with the shrapnel effect caused by the exploding plastic case.

Bullet hits usually occur (dramatically) in the chest or shoulder and consequently the most difficult areas to protect are the underside of the face and the insides of the arms. Designs for bullet plates must take this into consideration. Usually it is wise to ensure that an overhang of the metal plate adequately shields the face however far forward the actor inclines and that the arms are protected by costume sleeves of suitable thickness.

Blood
Bullet hits on the body must first rupture the clothing and then produce a flow of blood. To do so the bullet hit must be positioned just under the clothing. The blood comes from a rubber sac (a balloon will do) placed behind the bullet hit. It is a mistake to place the bullet hit behind the blood sac as this usually prevents the clothing from rupturing.

Operation
It is quite feasible for an actor to detonate bullet-hits on his own body by having a switch secreted in some part of his clothing. This method does, however, sometimes cause the actor to react prematurely. It is generally better if the effect can be operated by an effects man out of shot. Wires down the trousers terminating in a small two pin connector can be coupled to a line on the floor.

Viewpoint
It is not easy to show both the gun being fired and the bullets striking the body in the same frame unless the gun too is wired up and fired simultaneously with the bullet hits.

A pyrofuse and black powder charge in the gun barrel suffice for a single shot.

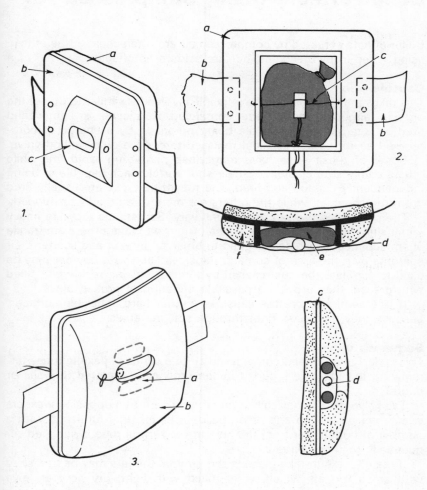

BULLET EFFECTS ON PEOPLE

1. Bullet plate
The plate is so designed that the body, particularly the underside of the chin and face, is completely shielded from flying pieces of plastic detonator. a, Plastic foam padding. b, Metal bullet plate. c, Shielded hole to accommodate bullet hit.

2. Bullet plate with large blood sac
a, Metal plate. b, Strap. c, Nylon cord. d, Actor's clothing. e, Blood sac. f, Plastic foam.

3. Alternative version
This type uses plastic foam instead of the shielded hole to trap the flying debris. a, Blood capsules. b, Plastic foam. c, Metal plate. d, Bullet hit.

Bullet Effects Using Compressed Air

Bullet effects actuated by compressed air are often cheaper than those using wired-in pyrotechnics, but are seldom as effective.

Capsule gun

This takes many forms, but the principle involved is similar to that of the ordinary airgun. A metal barrel containing a projectile is sighted and fired at a target, the projectile being propelled by a charge of compressed air (or carbon dioxide) released through a quick-action valve.

Some of these guns have magazines permitting rapid fire while others comprise a cluster of single-shot barrels each capable of being independently sighted and fired. The magazine types are usually fired 'from the shoulder' while the others are more often rigidly positioned.

The projectiles used in these guns vary. Sometimes they are heavy metal slugs to shatter bottles, vases or mirrors while others are fragile pharmaceutical capsules designed to break on impact and scatter their contents over the area of contact. Capsules filled with powder may be used to simulate the dust caused by a bullet striking rock while, filled with grease, they provide a passable imitation of broken glass.

It is essential to fire the capsules only at hard, inflexible surfaces, because they may pass right through soft materials.

Sequence valve

This is designed to feed compressed air to a series of flexible tubes terminating in hidden jets buried in the ground or secreted in walls or doors.

The valve itself is basically a metal tube with two opposing washers which can be slid up and down inside a larger tube furnished with a number of outlets. Air from the hole in the central tube is supplied sequentially to these outlets.

If the effect is to take place in the ground, the jets may be furnished with small funnels which, when filled with light, dry powder, give several puffs without the need for replenishment, the remaining powder falling back down the funnels and re-covering the jets.

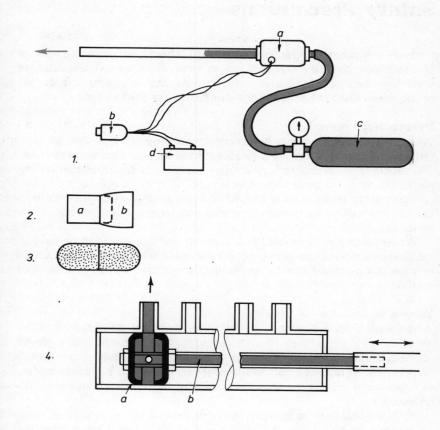

BULLET EFFECTS USING COMPRESSED AIR

1. Single barrel compressed-air gun
Also known as the capsule gun. a, Solenoid valve. b, Control button. c, Compressed air. d, Battery.

2. Metal projectile
a, Projectile. b, Skirt made from adhesive tape. The skirt expands in the barrel to form an airtight seal.

3. Gelatine capsule projectile
Both types of projectile are loaded via the barrel and pushed down with a rod. The gelatine capsule needs a wad of cotton wool behind it.

4. Sequence valve
This enables the compressed air to be fed sequentially to pipes buried in the ground. It provides an economical burst of machine gun fire. a, Two opposing cup washers. b, Sliding piston.

Safety Precautions

One of the most dangerous aspects of effects work is the use of pyrotechnics and explosives. It would seem unnecessary therefore to underline the need for suitable safeguards, but accidents sometimes occur even when all precautions appear to have been taken.

Pyrotechnic material
When working with loose pyrotechnic mixtures, ensure that all containers are closed or covered. Keep amounts to the minimums required and divide large amounts into smaller containers. Use non-ferrous implements to avoid producing sparks.

Don't store pyrotechnics that have been specially designed for particular jobs, unless their characteristics and formulae are shown on the container.

When testing experimental work do so under conditions as near to those finally envisaged as possible. What seems reasonable when fired in a sunlit, open field may be extremely dangerous at close quarters in a studio.

Wiring up
When wiring up a sequence of ground explosions, carefully mark the wires by tying sequences of knots at either end of single leads. Never connect anything to a wire without first making certain that the battery or firing box is not attached to the other end. It is not sufficient merely to disconnect one pole; somebody kicking the leads could cause reconnection.

In a well-laid-up sequence using conventional components, it is seldom necessary to test the circuit before firing, but if in doubt, use a detonator circuit tester which indicates satisfactory connections on a meter.

Flammables
When using gasoline for fire sequences apply it from containers with nozzles. Ensure that flammable liquids are not spilled or splashed onto clothing. Keep all containers well away from the scene of fire. Ensure that fire-fighting equipment is placed at strategic places. No fire effect, however small, should be carried out without at least one extinguisher available on site.

Where garments are to be set on fire, wet blankets extinguish the blaze more effectively than conventional fire extinguishers.

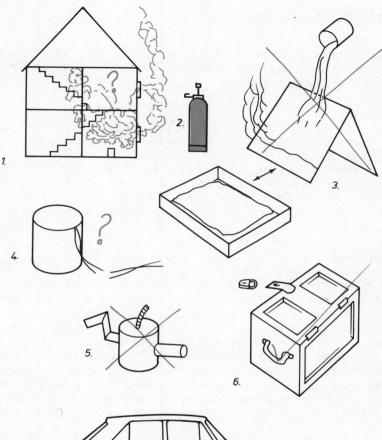

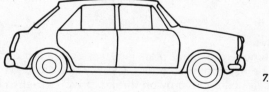

SAFETY PRECAUTIONS

1. Ensure that personnel cannot be trapped in buildings or studios before commencing fire and smoke sequences.

2. Keep fire extinguishers ready during fire sequences.

3. Don't pour liquid fuel onto something that has just been extinguished. Use pre-soaked material.

4. Always ensure that leads are not connected to firing devices before connecting explosive items.

5. Don't retain 'special' pyrotechnic items.

6. Always carry explosives and pyrotechnics in suitable containers.

7. It is usual for two people to accompany large amounts of explosives or pyrotechnics being transported by road. In the event of a breakdown one can summon help while the other remains with the vehicle.

Arrows

Four methods of making arrows appear to fly and to stick into their targets (usually human) are given here. The techniques explained may also be applied to knives and spears.

Whip pan
This method relies upon camera work, but with suitable sound effects it can seem remarkably convincing. It also has the advantages of supreme simplicity and economy of effort.

An arrow is fixed into its target. (If human, a body-plate with a small tube to hold the arrow is required.) The camera is pointed at a position from whence the arrow is supposed to come. On 'action' the camera is panned rapidly across the scene, stopping dead when framed up on the arrow.

Flight line
An aluminium tube provided with flight-feathers is threaded onto a thin nylon line. One end of this line is fastened to the target and the other end is held taut by a length of anchored elastic. The 'arrow' may be fired along this line by a hand-held catapult or sling shot. Instead of the customary sling however, the elastic should have a small s-shaped hook which can be inserted into the end of the tube.

To prevent it bouncing back the tube must be provided with a suitable restrainer when it comes to the end of its flight. A nail fastened to the tube can be made to stick into a block of balsa wood for some set-ups, but this should not be used on an actor as a breaking nylon line would endanger him. A spring loaded trap in the clothing is sometimes used.

Spring-up arrow
An arrow fastened to a body plate and spring-loaded to fly up when released may be used to good effect. Usually this device is operated by the actor himself pulling on a nylon thread. It works well in busy scenes and where actors can spin round as the arrow flies up. It is possible to hide the arrow in the clothing. This technique may also be used where an arrow or spear is apparently shot into a tree or part of the scenery.

Reverse filming
One well-known trick is to pull an arrow out of something and by reversing the film in printing make it appear to be going in. To get a good straight snatch on the arrow it is a good idea to tie it to a light nylon line which has its other end tied to a long length of elastic.

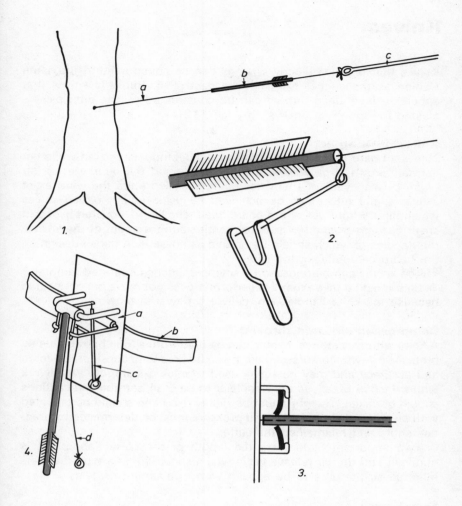

ARROWS

1. Flight line
a, Thin nylon line. b, Tubular arrow. c, Elastic rope. The tree is the target. The elastic rope holds the flight line taut.

2. Firing device
The arrow can be projected along the flight line by an ordinary catapult or sling shot with a hook to insert into the end of the tube.

3. Bounce trap
To prevent a tubular arrow from bouncing back, a simple rubber-washer trap can be set under the actor's clothing.

4. Fly-up arrow
a, Metal plate. b, Strap. c, Elastic spring. d, Release cord.

Knives

Knives that produce bloody wounds can be constructed in the same fashion as the dagger explained on page 116. Similarly knives that appear to have been thrown can be constructed on the principle explained for spring-up arrows on page 112.

Knife-throwing act

This is a board in front of which stands a beautiful circus girl while her partner throws large knives or hatchets around the perimeter of her body. In the event of there not being a skilled knife throwing artist available, the effect can be achieved by using spring-loaded knives which flip up from out of the board itself. The board, covered by a thin sheet of foam-plastic has slits to permit free movement of the knives, the handles of which should be as thin as possible. A garish design on the board camouflages the slits.

The knives can be released by solenoid catches operated remotely.

Care must be taken that the performer does not move out of position because the knife handles can deliver a powerful blow.

Compressed air knife thrower

A knife with a cylindrical handle can be fired from a 'gun barrel' tube by propelling it with compressed air. It can be fired with considerable force and accuracy and may be safely used to stick a knife into woodwork within inches of an actor. Needless to say, all sensible precautions should be taken. The gun must be rigidly fixed and should be provided with an efficient sight. Correct air pressure must be determined by practice shots and maintained thereafter.

Two important factors are the length of the barrel (about 5ft is nominal) and the air release valve which should be of a type that permits full air-pressure to be applied with a minimum of delay.

Safe knives

Knives cast in latex from plaster moulds may be used for fight scenes where safety of artistes is important.

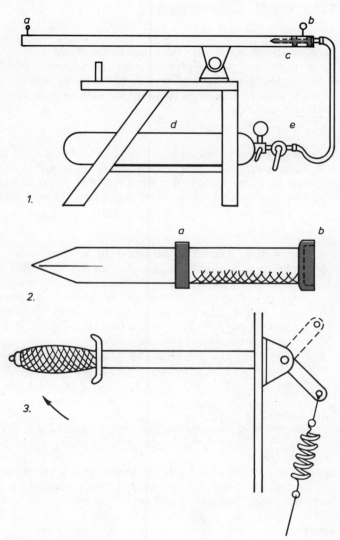

KNIVES

1. Compressed air knife thrower
a, Foresight. b, Backsight. c, Knife. d, Compressed air. e, Operating valve.

2. Knife for compressed air thrower
a, Piston washer. b, Cup washer. The scale is indicated above. The 'barrel' of the thrower is generally about 5ft long.

3. Spring-up knife
An alternative method is to conceal a flat dummy knife in a thin slot suitably camouflaged. A spring mechanism flips the knife upward when required.

Swords and Daggers

Property knives and daggers with retractable blades are simple to construct, but swords and rapiers present many problems. When in the course of the action these have to appear to be thrust into an actor's body it is nearly always necessary to adopt suitable camera viewpoints and sympathetic editing.

Dagger

The blade, spring-loaded to retract into the handle, should have parallel sides and a short, blunt point. This is necessary to ensure that the tip of the blade can be lost from sight in the thickness of clothing. Blood, contained in a piston in the handle can be made to flow down a tube concealed in the blade.

Fixed dagger

A shallow, slot-shaped container attached to a plate worn under clothing will receive a sawn-off dagger for scenes in which such a weapon is supposedly stuck into a human body. It is not very practical for the insertion to be undertaken as part of the action. It is better to fix the dagger beforehand and for the action to be mimed, shielded from the camera by the victim's body. Then, when he falls the implanted dagger can be seen protruding from the body.

   An alternative method and one which calls for only a small hole to be made in the clothing is to fix a threaded spigot to the sawn-off blade which is screwed into a threaded boss harnessed to the body.

Retractable sword

A parallel blade, made in two parts can be constructed so that the lower half slides out of sight behind the upper half. The blade should be dark grey to disguise the join.

   A flexible steel rule can be made to retract into a container fitted behind the handle and guard of a rapier, but best results are achieved on film by withdrawing the sword and reversing the action in printing.

Blood spurt

A dagger made from metal, or glass fibre and resin, can be fitted with a hollow rubber handle containing imitation blood. A fine-bore stainless-steel tube secreted in the blade allows the 'blood' to be discharged as required. This is a useful implement when the blade has to be drawn across some part of the body, leaving a bleeding gash.

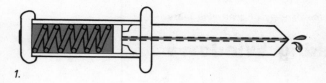

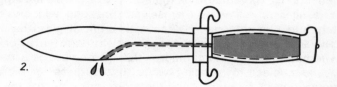

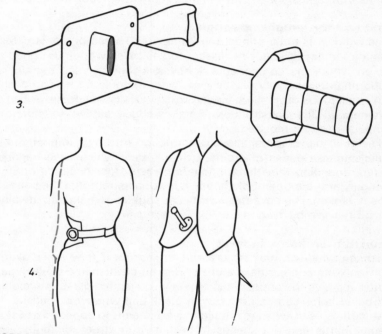

SWORDS AND DAGGERS

1. Stabbing knife
The blade is retractable and the piston handle squirts 'blood' from the point of the blade.

2. Cutting knife
When the rubber handle is squeezed, 'blood' flows from the knife edge.

3. Dagger socket
Worn under the clothing, such a socket holds a sawn-off dagger.

4. Penetration tube
Body flesh can be pulled in between the rib-cage and the hip. A tube is inserted in the space and the clothing packed out around it. A sword can then be thrust through the tube.

Avoiding the dangers of shattering glass.

Breaking Windows

Many effects rely more upon the manner in which they are staged than on the devices or materials themselves. Breaking windows fall very definitely into this category. Seldom can artificial glass be produced perfectly clear and yet be safe enough not to harm an actor or stunt man who has to come into contact with it. 'Soft glass' is usually thick, yellow and subject to warping while 'brittle glass' can break into dangerously sharp splinters. It is, therefore, often necessary to shoot scenes from a position where the glass cannot be seen in close detail.

Windows for jumping through

If the window is multi-paned, the framework should be constructed of ordinary lumber (it is not necessary to use balsa wood), designed in a fashion where the components lightly slot together and remain self-supporting. Break-away plastic glass panes should be held in position with small blobs of putty or modelling-clay. Nails should never be used anywhere in the construction. Small wedges suffice to stiffen the framework where required.

The glass panes in the above construction smash on impact, but it is feasible to use panes of ordinary clear plastic which have been pre-broken. Providing that the window is viewed from one side or is first seen only at the moment of impact, it is not apparent that the panes are already broken. The advantage of this arrangement is that all the pieces can be reassembled and re-used.

Simulated broken windows

Unbroken windows may be dressed to look as if they are broken by applying various dressing materials. Broken plastic sheets, black paper and tin foil give the appearance of holes and jagged glass, while cracks and bullet holes can be drawn with black and white wax pencils. This stratagem is used when real buildings are meant to appear derelict and enables battle and riot scenes to be filmed in street locations.

Shock wave

Where a window has to appear to break by shock or blast, it can be arranged by fitting sheets of breakaway glass into special window frames. These are provided with slotted rods which grip the bottoms of the panes of glass. When rotated by hidden levers the rods distort the glass to breaking point.

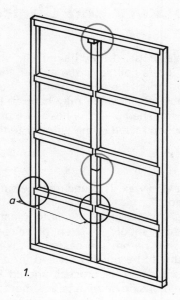

1.

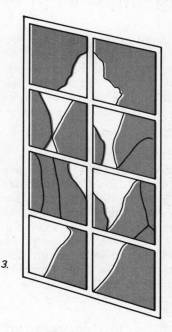

3.

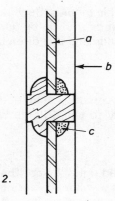

2.

BREAKING WINDOWS

1. Windows to be broken (or for stunt men to leap through) can be constructed in a way that allows them to be reassembled for re-takes. a, Glazing bar fitted very loosely.

2. Detail of window construction. a, Breaking glass. b, Direction of impact. c, Modelling clay.

3. Clear plastic resin sheet in the form of pre-broken panes can be assembled as shown. If the action is filmed and edited so that the 'glass' is seen only from the moment of impact it appears to be breaking.

Breaking Bottles, Crockery and Chairs

It is not always easy to make breakable props. If they have to be sufficiently fragile to break or come apart in the course of the action, they invariably present problems when actors have to handle them beforehand. Typical of this is a breakable chair which may have to be substantially weakened to break when smashed over the head of a performer and yet must not fall to pieces when raised in the air prior to the attack.

Bottles

Those used in fight scenes should be cast in wax. This ensures the safety of the actors and stuntmen involved.

Wax bottles are made by pouring hot paraffin wax into plaster moulds. The moulds (usually two-piece) should be free of release agents and must be soaked in cold water before the casts are taken. Once the wax has been poured in it should be quickly swilled around and the mould stood upside down to drain. This process should be repeated three times. Standing the mould upside down ensures that the wax does not settle at the bottom and produce a dangerously thick base which could cause injury. Wax bottles may be varnished for added realism.

Bottles may also be cast in plaster from flexible moulds. Such bottles are useful where they have to be thrown about or shot up by gun-fire. Bottles of plastic must be made in special moulds and it is often better to purchase them ready-made.

Cups, saucers and vases

These are frequently cast in shell-plaster, but even dry plaster does not always break as desired. It is often necessary to score items with a sharp knife beforehand.

Chairs and stools

These may be made from balsa wood or foamed rigid-plastic. The best of these is a variety of polyurethane which has a yellow colour not unlike that of wood. If balsa is used it should be selected for its softness. Some grades of balsa can be very hard and tough.

Nails and screws should never be used in the construction of breakables. Joints should be cemented.

If they are required for fight sequences, balsa wood chairs and stools should have their seats constructed from an assembly of thin sheets. Again, pre-scoring of the material assists the break-up.

Plaster

Items may be constructed from a mixture of plaster and sawdust—a useful material for props which have to crumble rather than break.

BREAKING BOTTLES, CROCKERY AND CHAIRS

1. Wax bottles and crockery. a, Soak plaster mould in water and drain. b, Pour in hot wax and swill. c, Invert to drain wax.

2. Balsa breakaway furniture. Use sheet wood to fabricate heavy parts.

3. Breakaway chair of plastic polyurethane foam coated thinly with plaster of paris.

4. Ornaments, statues and other breakaway items can be cast in a mixture of sawdust and plaster.

Breaking and Collapsing Scenery

The scenic designer can assist the effects designer where breaking scenery is required if he incorporates suitable camouflage techniques in his designs. (For example, large areas of plain wall are difficult to deal with.) Textured or patterned wall papers enable pre-broken areas to be disguised.

Falling shelves
Very often shelves that fall have one end fixed and the other end free. It is a simple matter to remove a peg from behind which has been hidden in the thickness of the shelf. Alternatively, if the shelf is hinged to the wall it drops forward when a retaining thread is released. This can be hidden between items on the shelf.

Brick walls
Walls can be assembled from bricks cut from expanded polystyrene. Fuller's earth shaken on the courses of bricks as the wall is assembled provides realistic dust when it falls. These bricks are suitable for comedy programmes, but are not heavy enough to look authentic. Weighted by the insertion of lead or metal slugs and coated with liquid latex they fall more realistically but do not damage the studio floor – or such things as automobiles which may have to be driven into them.

Collapsing floor
One of the greatest problems where large areas of floor have to collapse is the fact that the weight of the floor tends to jam any release mechanism. Devices that enable the floor to be dropped easily and yet support heavy weights are shown opposite. The toggle collapses easily once it has been opened past its straight line position, but it requires a powerful initial snatch to open it. The wheeled foot is a good device if the weight has to be dropped by remote control. A solenoid-bomb release may be used to free the supporting line.

 The roller is very simple and light to operate. It can be operated by a line tied to the handle, but it does require that the support is able to drop clear once it has left the roller.

Mine shaft collapse
Large pieces of expanded polystyrene covered with cloth and latex can be painted to resemble rock. Sawdust and peat adequately simulate falling earth and shale.

 A breaking pit-prop can be constructed similarly to the toggle but where it has to be knocked away a small hidden wheel fitted inside the foot assists the action.

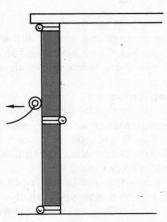

The support is 'broken' by pulling.

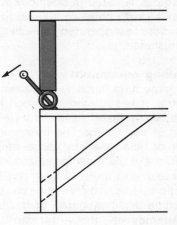

The support placed on a roller falls
away when roller is turned.

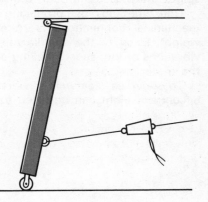

The support rolls away when the
bomb release frees the cord.

123

Popping Corks and Shaking Equipment

Comedy programme scripts sometimes call for corks that have to pop out of bottles. They also call for items of equipment that have to go beserk. Here are some methods of obtaining these effects.

Popping corks

If the bottle has to be hand-held it is possible to incorporate a small carbon dioxide dispenser in a glass-fibre reproduction bottle which when operated will pressurise a compartment containing liquid. The cork should be a reasonably tight fit in order that the pressure can build up before the liquid disgorges.

For a champagne bottle in an ice-bucket it is possible to instal the basic parts of an air-pistol in the truncated bottle. The plunger is first cocked by pushing a ramrod down the neck of the bottle. The device is then operated by pushing a lever secreted in the imitation ice.

Bottles situated in positions where they will not be touched can be provided with pipes connected to either conventional soda-syphons or, for more exaggerated effects, pressurised water or foam fire-extinguishers.

Shaking equipment

If a large item, such as a washing machine, has to go violently out of control, it is sometimes a good idea to fix it to a sub-baseboard. The prop can be fastened to the baseboard by large coil springs of the type used in upholstery. The baseboard can then either be secured to the floor or held down by stage-weights.

To make the machine shudder an electric motor fitted with a suitable gear box and cranked arm can be used to impart the necessary oscillations. The arm should be passed through the bottom of the washing machine and connected to the baseboard.

Alternatively, the motor can be fitted with a cam in contact with a spigot that passes through the bottom of the machine.

One method of producing vibrations without any external mechanical connections is to equip the motor with an off-centre weight. Fixed to the spindle the weight produces either high speed vibrations or low speed shaking according to its size and the power of the motor.

To show an alarm clock vibrating madly as the bell goes off, the eccentric weight can be fitted to the spring mechanism.

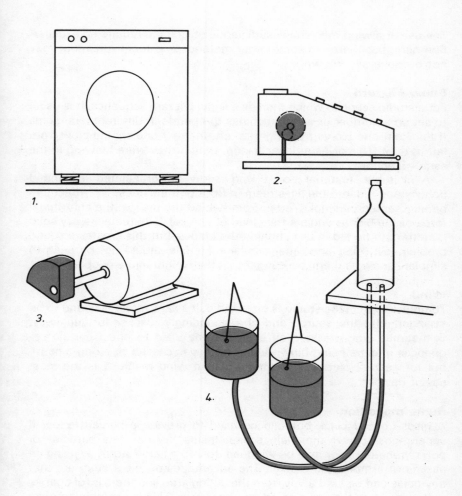

SHAKING EQUIPMENT

1. Large items that have to shake should be mounted on springs.
2. A motorised arm and crank will vibrate small items.
3. An eccentric weight on a motor shaft produces violent oscillation.
4. Two chemicals that will foam on being mixed may be introduced into a bottle by lifting the containers.

125

Wind and Blizzards

The use of a wind machine is sufficiently obvious to require no explanation here, but there are some other methods and techniques that may not be generally known.

Snow blizzard
For a studio scene in which there is a snow blizzard sequence, it is usual to set up a number of wind machines to operate in different directions. If the front one blows from right to left, the rear one should blow from left to right. This gives a richer texture than if they were blowing in the same direction.

A suitable material for driven snow is granulated expanded polystyrene fed into the air-stream in front of the blades. The effect can be augmented by smoke fed in from behind the blades (the centrifugal force of the blades widens the cloud of smoke). Where necessary solid material can be fed in from behind the blades, but this creates a sound problem. Sawdust and other similar materials should not be used to simulate snow as there is a danger that they might injure peoples' eyes.

Wind
To depict wind in the studio is often difficult as any effect is bound to be stronger near the source and correspondingly weaker further away. Sometimes high pressure air lines may be used to effect certain sequences (papers being blown about or leaves cascading along a path), but for general purposes the multi-bladed wind machine is the most useful device.

Superimposition
A glass-fronted black box can be used to provide a blizzard effect if superimposed over the main scene. Inside the box fine particles of polystyrene or paper may be whipped up into a fierce storm by using an air line or a motorised blower. The advantages of this system are that any noise can be kept away from the acting area and there is, of course, no loose material to be cleared up afterwards. This is useful in comedy shows where there is no time for involved scene changes.

Film loop
Expanded polystyrene granules blown about in front of a black background may be filmed and used later as superimposition material for scenes in the studio where a real blizzard would be impractical. Smoke blown and filmed in the same fashion can be used to resemble a sand storm, but this is more dramatic if filmed by an 'undercranked' camera to double the speed of the action.

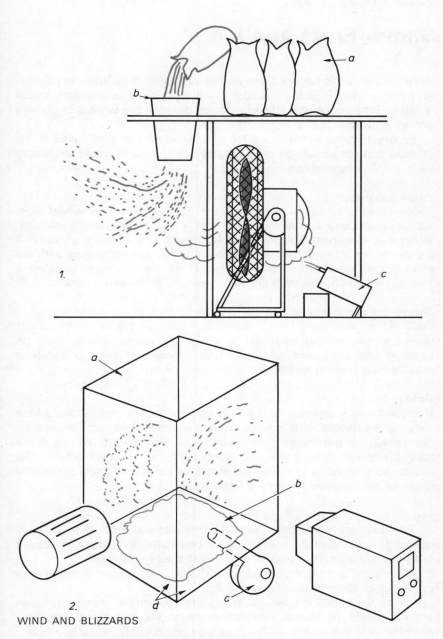

WIND AND BLIZZARDS

1. Set-up for sustained blizzard sequence
a, Bags of expanded polystyrene. b, Hopper. c, Smoke gun.

2. Superimposition snow box
A, Black backing. b, Cloth bottom. c, Blower. d, Glass. The cloth must be agitated throughout the action. This is best done by moving the blower.

Cold effects in a warm studio.

Snow, Frost and Ice

Snow in the studio causes more problems than may be apparent. Salt is commonly used in some studios, but although it has excellent visual qualities it has corrosive effects that can damage the wheels of camera dollies and other equipment.

Expanded-polystyrene granules and sawdust are both used in TV studios, but they must be of a suitably fire-retardent grade to comply with the fire regulations.

Falling snow
This is invariably finely shredded paper or polythene dispensed from special motorised containers hung above the action. One such container has a curved bottom in which there is a number of slots. A motor-driven, rotating rod has a series of spikes corresponding with the slots. These collect the shredded paper as they revolve, carrying it through the slots, where it flutters down in measured amounts.

Snow on the ground
To build up sufficient depth, sandbags may be placed in the areas where actors are not required to walk. This build up can then be covered with sawdust which in turn is covered with polystyrene granules or white powder.

Frost
If property or scenic items are first sprayed with a water-based glue they can be dusted with a white powder to resemble frost. The powder can usually be purchased commercially, but a substitute can be made from powdered mica, chalk and wood pulp. On windows where frost has to be cleared in vision use methylated spirit and finely powdered chalk or talc applied as a very light spray.

Ice
For ice that has to be broken on the surface of water paraffin wax may be used. If possible the water should be heated and hot wax poured onto the surface. Wax poured onto cold water sets badly.

For icicles, pieces of twisted polythene can be dipped into hot wax or polyester resin and hung up to set.

Large simulated ice blocks are difficult to make, but techniques where sheets of heated and distorted acrylic plastic are welded together and then filled with water give remarkably realistic effects.

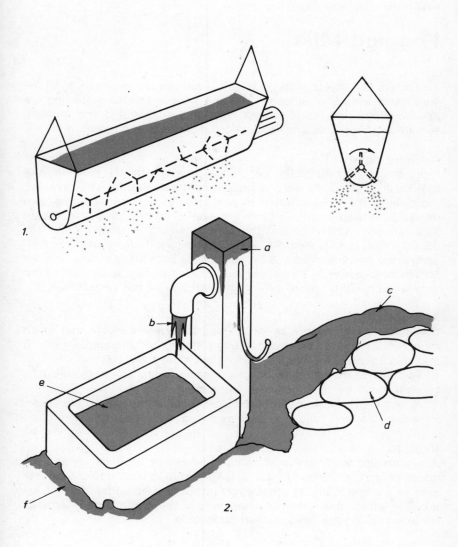

SNOW, FROST AND ICE

Ice and snow effects must usually be applied in such a way that they do not permanently damage scenery or props.

1. Snow dropping box
This motorised unit has a spiked revolving rod which distributes shredded paper through the slots in the trough.

2. Frozen prop
a, Applied frost. b, Resin icicles. c, Cloth covered in saw-dust. d, Sandbags to build up drifts. e, Wax ice. f, Heaped polystyrene granules.

Fog and Mist

To achieve the effects of fog or mist it is not always necessary to fill the studio with clouds of smoke. There are various aids to producing the desired effect, but each has its own applications and the problem should be thoroughly analysed before a method is chosen.

A foggy night
Night scenes provide better conditions than day for the simulation of fog. The dark backgrounds give greater contrast with the white swirling fog or mist and make it easier to see. Low key lighting also helps and this is more easily achieved in night scenes than in day. A moderate application of smoke behind the action gives a suitable effect if all back-lighting is switched off. A similar amount in front of the action completes the picture and as far as possible both areas should be front lit. The smoke should be passed over dry-ice to cool it and the studio ventilation system turned off for the duration of the sequence.

A foggy day
Conditions are the same as for the night sequence except that much more smoke has to be used. Lighting should be arranged so that it bounces back off the smoke rather than shines through it.

To enhance the effect, nylon gauze (easily obtainable from stockings or tights) can be stretched over the camera lens.

A reasonable illusion can be created by superimposing a previously filmed fog effect — this is known as a 'fog loop'. (see below)

Vignette
A vignette of white material placed in front of the lens softens the edges of the picture and by causing light to flare back into the camera creates a degraded image that augments smoke and other devices used. The effect must not be used where the camera pans around, because the treated area is then noticeable.

Superimposed effects
A reasonable illusion can be created by superimposing the effect. One of the best sources of superimposition is the fog loop. Smoke filmed against a black background can be superimposed over the main picture to give a realistic effect, but as it is slow moving it is impracticable to use the loop effect when rapid pans or cuts are necessary in the sequence. Cuts can be accepted if the final recording can be edited so that there is an appropriate 'jump' in the fog at the time of the change of viewpoint, but panning makes the fog appear to race across the picture.

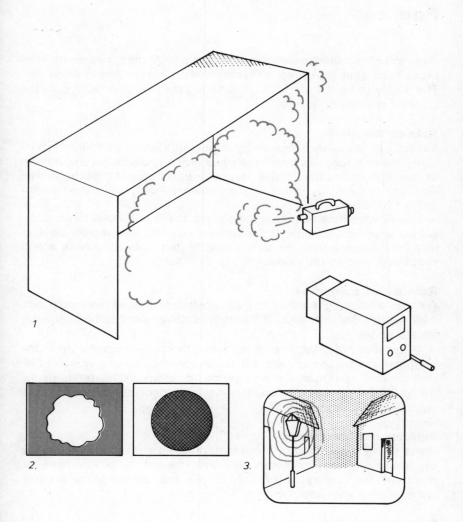

FOG AND MIST

1. Fog retainer
A light scenic construction can be erected to localise and retain smoke used for fog effects. It should have an open weave muslin roof or a plastic sheet to allow the scene to be lit.

2. Effects filters
Various filters may be used over the camera lens to soften or fog the scene.

3. Lamps for emphasis
A street lamp helps to establish the presence of fog or mist.

Rain

Rain, which so often interferes with location filming, can sometimes prove to be almost as great a nuisance when it is created in the studio. The problems lie not so much in producing the rain as in dealing with it when it reaches floor level.

Rain in the studio
Falling rain is usually achieved by arranging a series of drilled water--pipes over the scene below. Fixed pipes give an obviously static pattern of rain and to counteract this, alternate pipes must be gently rocked back and forth. A low-speed wind-machine, suitably positioned, adds a touch of realism.

Where long runs of tube are installed, the drilled holes nearest the supply spurt fiercely while those furthest away do little more than dribble. To overcome this, the pipes must be fed from both ends and, if necessary, also in the middle.

Rain down a window
A sheet of clear rigid plastic or glass positioned behind the studio window suffices for this effect if a length of drilled water pipe is suitably angled at the top.

If the sheet of glass is framed, a trough can be constructed in the bottom of the frame to collect the water. It is then an easy matter to install a small, electrically driven pump to return the water from the trough to the pipe at the top, allowing the effect to run continuously without supervision.

Exterior rain sequences
These are best achieved by using high-pressure hoses squirted into the air. It is not always necessary to drown the actors, as rain between them and the camera can, if skilfully directed, appear to be in depth while leaving the actors dry.

Rain loop
Simulated rain filmed in a studio against a black background can later be superimposed over studio scenes. It is essential to make this rain gust about during the pre-filming (a wind machine will suffice) so that when camera panning takes place in the studio, the rain does not appear to act unnaturally. This technique is ideal for shows where it would be impractical to use real water.

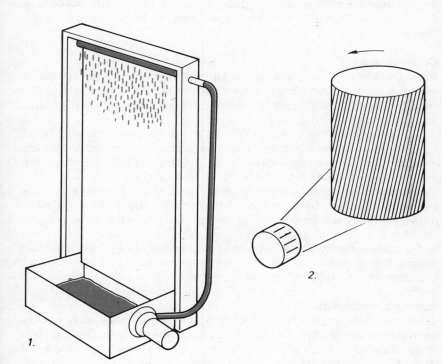

RAIN

1. Rain on windows
Placed behind studio windows this rain effect can be left to run without attention.

2. Background rain
Narrow stripes painted on the transparent cylinder of the 'flamedrum' provide a stylised rain effect that can be projected onto background screens.

Better and quicker than nature.

Cobwebs

Artificial cobwebs placed strategically in dingy interior scenes provide an atmosphere that would be difficult to achieve in any other way. These cobwebs, usually latex-based, are sprayed from a hand-held dispenser.

Cobweb gun

Basically, the cobweb dispenser is an electric motor on the spindle of which is fitted a cylindrical reservoir containing the latex solution. It is sealed with a flat plate held in position on the spindle by an adjustable nut.

The fit between the plate and the lip of the container must be good, because it is from this gap that the latex is spun in the form of threads. If the plate is screwed down too tightly no filaments emerge, whereas if the gap is too great, latex spins out in messy gobs.

The fan fitted behind the container blows the latex filaments onto the set. Its blades can be constructed from thick rubber sheet or, alternatively, they may be formed of metal and protected by a suitable guard.

For convenience, some cobweb-guns operate on low voltage. This means that they can be run from the power supply, via a step-down transformer, or they can be run from batteries.

Applying cobwebs

Latex cobwebs remain sticky for some time and while being applied they adhere readily to most surfaces and to themselves. Nevertheless to get them to build up in an open space it is necessary to provide some type of framework. Usually it is sufficient to string fine cotton threads across the void. In most cases these may be severed after they have done their job and allowed to go limp.

Where it is difficult to build up very large amounts of cobwebs, the work can be speeded up by using the spun plastic filaments used for Christmas decorations. These can be teased out and hung about the set.

Latex cobwebs should be dusted liberally with talcum-powder when the spraying is complete. This makes them more visible and the fall-out powder suitably complements the scene.

The mixture

Some latex preparations may be used without modification, but others have to be diluted to render them thin enough to spin properly. Care must be taken when using these substances as some are sufficiently inflammable to contravene studio fire regulations.

134

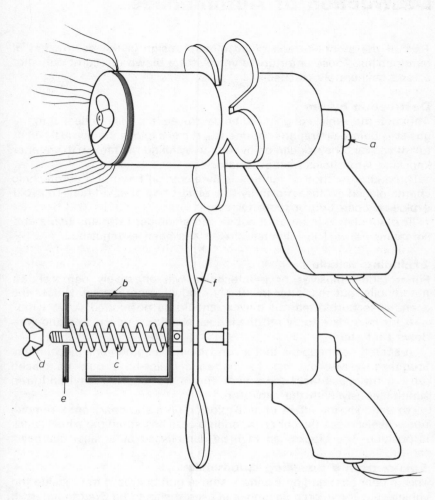

COBWEBS

The cobweb gun has three main parts. The motor, which is mounted in a suitable handle, the cylinder containing the cobweb solution and the fan blade that blows the filaments onto the set. a, Operating switch. b, Latex container. c, Spring. d, Wing nut. e, Sealing plate. f, Rubber-bladed fan.

Destruction of Automobiles

Part of the stock-in-trade of an effects design is the destruction of automobiles. These unfortunate vehicles are blown up, burnt out, shot at and deliberately crashed.

Destruction by fire

Although the vehicle is going to be destroyed it is wise to deal with the gas tank before operations commence. It can explode dangerously if left full of vapour. The risk can be overcome by filling the tank with water or knocking large holes in the bottom.

A popular method of ignition is by electrical firing of a pyrotechnic charge placed in close proximity to a plastic bag of liquid fuel. To avoid explosion open two or more windows.

The upholstery in an automobile can smoulder for many hours and sometimes a vehicle reignites after it has been extinguished.

Exploding vehicle

Either high-explosives or pyrotechnics will effectively demolish an automobile, but the latter invariably produce more smoke. Unless the scene is to be blotted out the car should be positioned down wind.

If the doors are to fly off, the hinges should be unscrewed and windows kept shut.

It sometimes happens that a windshield flies out in one piece. If it is toughened glass, but has to shatter, a bullet-hit should be placed against the glass (held there by a chunk of modelling-clay) and fired simultaneously with the explosion.

To enhance the effect of an explosion on a stationary auto, remove two wheels, place the car on wooden blocks and stand the wheels back in position. The blocks can then be demolished by smaller charges.

Smoke from a travelling automobile

This is best arranged by having a smoke gun operated from inside the vehicle, but if pyrotechnic smoke is used it should be fixed to a part of the vehicle (or mounted on an outrigger) well away from the gas-tank vent.

Steam from the radiator

Use a can or stout plastic bottle that can be sealed. The cap should be provided with a quarter-inch hole.

To operate the effect, fill the can two-thirds full with hot water and add several small pieces of dry ice. Screw the cap down and position the can near the radiator. A jet of harmless 'steam' shoots up from the hole. Useful when scalded arms or faces are called for.

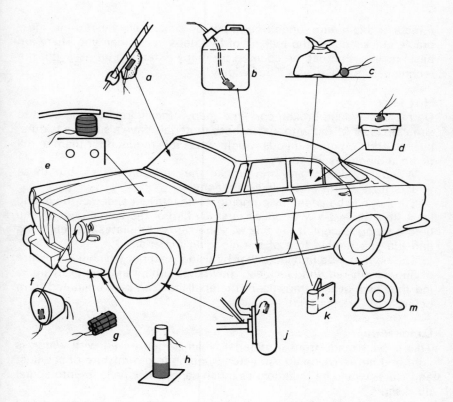

DESTRUCTION OF AUTOMOBILES

a, Bullet-hit held to windshield with block of clay. b, plastic canister containing gasoline and sealed pyrotechnic explosive to create a big fire effect. c, smaller fire effect using plastic bag of fuel and thunderflash. d, smaller still, a plastic bucket of fuel with an igniter suspended above. e, a ground-maroon will fling open bonnet lid. f, bullet effect on lamp glass using bullet hit. g, high explosive placed under or in car for big blow-up. h, mortar placed to one side will lift and overturn vehicle. j, bullet hits inserted into tyre fired via slip-rings mounted inside wheel can be used while vehicles in motion. k, hinges should have their screws removed if pyrotechnic explosion is used in vehicle. m, a tyre cast in latex can be used for comedy flat sequence.

Lava, Quicksand and Swamps

Effects of this nature range from a person sinking slowly into the 'inexorable quicksand' to the making of footsteps in wet cement. There are basic recipes that can be adapted for many different purposes, but the techniques for their use differ widely.

Hot lava

Oatmeal, sawdust, broken cork and many other things can be used to simulate lava. Mixed with water these materials have a suitable texture, but the addition of sand adds weight when it is required for them to roll down a sloping surface.

Without 'red hot' ash and smoke they appear lifeless, but these effects have to be added independently.

Smoke may be added by pumping it into jets just ahead of the rolling lava. (It is always a wise policy to study film of the actual phenomena before trying to copy it.) In this way the smoke emulates the real thing and the jets remain free of the clogging material.

The heat can be implied either by using material which is a mixture of fluorescent-red and black ash (powdered rubber and oil) or by pouring the 'lava' over a translucent material that can be illuminated from below with orange light.

Quicksand

This is best made from a material which, when mixed with water, is light and non-enveloping. An actor plunging into a mixture of sawdust and water would be in almost as much danger as if he leapt into actual quicksand.

Quite often this effect can be achieved by floating cork chippings and cork dust on the surface of water. In this way a person can sink below the crust on the surface and swim away. Alternatively, a tank can be constructed which enables the character to raise his head under a false bank where he is able to breathe without problems, the assumption being that he has succumbed to the quicksand or swamp. An air line that can deliver bubbles to the place of immersion leads the viewer to believe that the character is breathing his last at the spot where he sank.

Swamps

Nasty swamp effects can be created by mixing water with Fuller's Earth until it has a soup-like consistency. Pieces of dry-ice thrown into this mixture not only cause it to bubble menacingly, but also produce sinister white vapour when the bubbles burst.

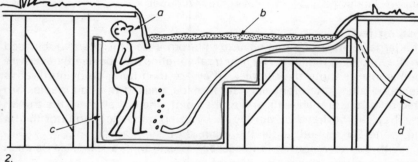

LAVA, QUICKSAND AND SWAMPS

1. Hot lava for model scenes can be created by using a heated base plate onto which is pushed a mixture of oil and sawdust. a, Model building. b, 'Lava' consisting of powdered rubber, oil and sawdust, pushed from behind. c, Heated steel plate.

2. A swamp into which an actor has to disappear can be constructed in the studio if a suitable tank or plastic lined wooden box is filled with water. The surface of the water should be covered with buoyant material such as cork granules. Where a large area of swamp is required it is usual to keep it shallow except for the spot where the man has to sink. a, Air space for actor. b, Cork and sawdust on surface. c, Heavy plastic sheet. d, Compressed air.

Some Special Plants

The products of horticulture and agriculture suffer severely at the hands of comedy writers. Here are some favourite gags.

Wilting flowers

A single plastic bloom fastened to a flexible tube can be made to wilt if a stiff wire, previously inserted in the tube, is slowly withdrawn from below. It is possible to reverse the action if the wire has a rounded end and the flower-stem does not kink in the wilted mode.

Falling blooms

A bloom that has to fall from a tree or plant can be electrically released if the bloom (as light as possible) is fitted with a tiny bar magnet. The branch from which it has to fall terminates in a soft-iron core (a nail will do) wound with 30 or 40 turns of insulated copper wire.

The bloom is offered up to the nail where it will remain in magnetic contact. However, when a low-voltage, high-amperage current is applied to the coil, the bloom falls. The polarity should, of course, oppose the magnet.

A reasonable number of blooms may be released in this way, but the supply leads must be of heavy-gauge copper wire.

Falling fruit

If a large number of items have to fall from a tree they can be released in the following manner: The fruit (real varieties may be used) have wire hooks inserted into their bodies. They are then hung on nylon threads secreted along the branches. The threads, passed through staples are tied off at the branch ends and at the point where they meet the trunk.

They can be freed by cutting or by using a plastic detonator (bullet hit, page 98) buried under the main knot.

With this technique it is necessary to use only a few lines as each thread supports several clusters of fruit.

Leaping flowers

Sometimes a flower is required to leap from its stem. This effect can be produced by fitting the bloom with a small hollow cap which slides easily over an appropriate metal tube. Soft copper is useful here.

A quick burst of compressed air causes the flower to fly off the stalk.

This system is not recommended for multiple effects unless each tube is independently fed.

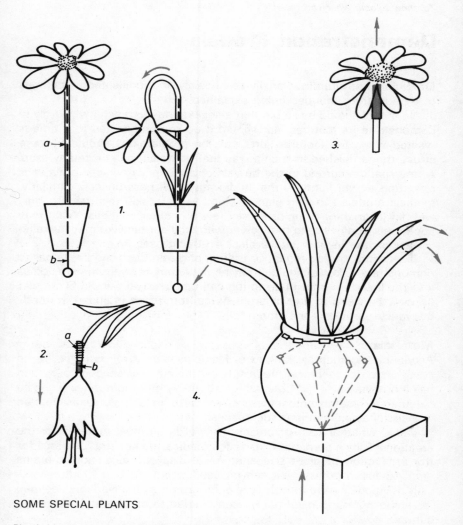

SOME SPECIAL PLANTS

Plastic blooms and leaves can generally be used, but for some effects (such as the leaping flower 3) blooms must be made from tissue paper.

1. Wilting flowers
A stiff wire in a plastic tube provides this comical effect. a, Plastic tubing. b, Stiff wire.

2. Falling bloom
Held by a magnet the blooms falls when the polarity is reversed. a, Electromagnet. b, Magnet.

3. Leaping flower
The lightweight bloom has a hollow cap fitting over a metal tube through which compressed air can be fed.

4. Wilting Aspidestra
Operated from below with nylon lines.

Demonstration Models

Educational programmes on TV rely heavily on models and animations to demonstrate theories being explained.

No model should be so big that a speaker has to reach awkwardly to demonstrate its features, nor should it be so complicated that time is wasted while the lecturer sorts out the problems. It should be constructed and finished in such a way that the result can be clearly seen. A tiny spark occurring in the bowels of a complicated set-up which is reflecting all the lights in the studio may well pass unseen. Similarly, medical models showing glands, blood vessels, skin textures etc. may well fail to make any point if they rely on colour changes. What may appear perfectly clear to the viewer with a colour receiver may make no impact on the viewer with a black-and-white set.

If a demonstration model consisting of glass tubes and flasks has to demonstrate a flow of liquid it may be necessary to inject foreign bodies into the liquid in order that motion can be observed. Air bubbles show up well, but tend to find different paths from those intended. Neutral-buoyancy particles are better.

Materials

Acrylic plastic such as Perspex or Plexiglas is an ideal material for the construction of technical models. It can be cut and shaped easily and has a pristine finish not obtainable with many other materials. It can be coloured to resemble most metals, but unlike metal it can be assembled without heat or laborious techniques.

Latex, whether cast or cut from sheet is an ideal material for the creation of lifelike animal organs for medical demonstrations, but for the production of giant size anatomical displays (ears, noses, brains etc.) expanded polystyrene can be used.

Most models used for this type of programme are invariably destined for a short life and need not be constructed to great standards of accuracy.

Exaggeration

It occasionally happens that there is a conflict of opinion between the academic and the producer on the subject of veracity. Should a result be 'assisted' merely to demonstrate the point; The answer in most cases must surely be 'Yes'. There is little sense in showing something that the viewer will not see.

142

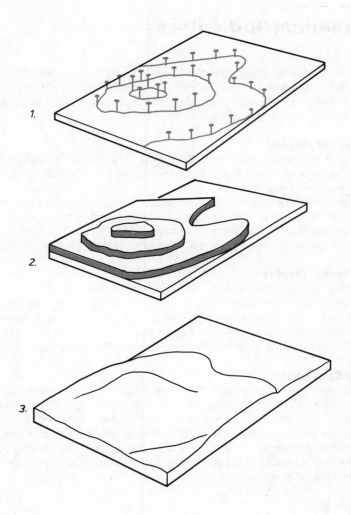

DEMONSTRATION MODELS

1. Topographical models or relief maps can be made by driving nails of different lengths along the contour lines.
2. Another method is to use sheets of expanded-polystyrene or soft-board to indicate the different levels.
3. The body of the map is then filled in with modelling clay or plaster, obtaining a gentle sweep between levels.

143

Numerical Indicators

There are many numerical displays and scoring devices available on the commercial market, but occasionally it is necessary for something to be custom-built to suit either the needs of the programme or for reasons of economy. A few ideas are given here.

Theatrical display
Each unit is constructed from 35 lamps arranged in a rectangle, five lamps wide and seven high. With this format it is possible to display every number from 0 to 9.

Each lamp must have an individual switching wire going to a selector unit that is designed to switch the groups of lamps necessary to produce the digits. This form of display looks better if placed behind a sheet of coloured plastic so that the unlit lamps cannot be seen.

Segmental display
This display uses the format now commonly associated with pocket calculator read-outs. It requires seven independently illuminated strips integrated in the form shown opposite. If each segment is illuminated by a single circuit then a switching unit with only seven individual contacts is required as against 35 contacts for the theatrical display.

Edge-lit display
This makes use of the fact that acrylic plastic has the property of transmitting light throughout its area without significant loss. Ten sheets of plastic are placed one behind the other, each being illuminated by an independent light source along one or more of its edges. The numerals are engraved into the material by drilling a series of blind holes into the plastic sheets. A switch unit with ten contacts is required for this display.

Switch unit
A suitable unit for use with any of the above can be constructed in either of two ways. The first uses a series of cams on a central shaft which operates either pairs of contacts or a bank of micro switches. The other uses a conductive cylinder which is lacquered with an insulating paint. (Even a beer can be used for this.) The paint is scraped away where rubbing strips are required to make contact.

144

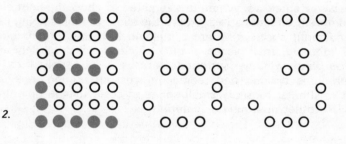

1.

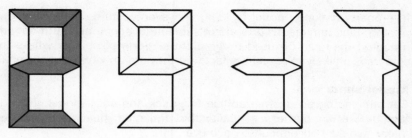

2.

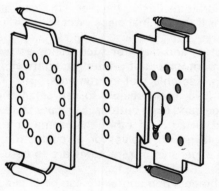

3.

NUMERICAL INDICATORS

1. Segmental display
A simple system needing only seven contacts on the switching unit.

2. Theatrical display
A more complicated construction needing thirty five contacts.

3. Edge-lit display
Acrylic plastic transmits light without significant loss and can be evenly illuminated by shining light through its edges. Numbers drilled in the form of blind holes then show up clearly. The edge tabs are bent when the sheets are made up in packs of ten.

Photographs on the Screen

In property making, model building and even costume embellishment, photographs may be used to effect substantial economies. Cut out and mounted they can be used to simulate all sorts of objects where the camera is unlikely to reveal the fact that they are only two-dimensional.

Model shots

Cut-out photographs often suffice for quick and easy model shots. In fact they often possess a quality that the most painstaking model-maker would find difficult to achieve.

For night shots the original photos should be taken in flat light to avoid give-away shadows. Where it is required to show the light coming from different directions (e.g. where the same model is being used for day and night shots or where a building is to be illuminated by flashes of lightning small pieces of three dimensional detail (chimney stacks, door and window surrounds, etc.) can be applied to the photograph. It is difficult and tedious to cut out around trees and bushes: It is simpler to apply small sprigs of scale foliage or tufts of steel wool or other appropriate materials.

Props

Items such as door furniture (locks, handles etc.) can quite often be applied as photographs if the original pieces would be difficult or expensive to use.

Other uses are meters and dials for such things as power-plant or aircraft-controls. The photographs if printed on lightweight paper, can be rear illuminated to resemble real instruments.

For costume work it is quite feasible to use small photographs to simulate medals, badges and even buttons. Similarly plates, ornaments, books, statuettes and all sorts of other things may be produced as photographs and displayed on shelves or in cupboards. This is particularly useful where expensive or rare items are to be used as dressing.

Photos of embellishments and engraving can be applied to weapons and works of art and photographic brass handles may be applied to coffins,– or safe deposit boxes to walls. The possibilities are endless.

PHOTOGRAPHS ON THE SCREEN

Photographs appear to be three-dimensional on the screen because they, like everything else in the picture, are seen only as two-dimensional objects. Provided they are used with discretion they will appear as detailed objects and not merely pieces of paper.

1. Photographic background and front of model. 2. Photograph of decoration for costume work. 3. Photograph of brass lock applied to chest. 4. Photographs of books and silver picture frame.

Remote Control

Commercially produced radio-control devices for use with model air-craft can be adapted to fire distant explosions. They are sometimes affected, however, by sources of stimulation other than the operator's own transmitter. To minimise this possibility, devices are designed to operate only when two different wavelengths are applied simultaneously.

Electric ignition
A novel and economic method of achieving remote operation is that in which a nylon supporting or restraining line is severed by heat. A pyrofuse (page 98) is inserted snugly into a small metal tube through which has been drilled a transverse hole. The nylon line is passed through this hole and the pyrofuse is pushed up against it so that the head is in contact with the line. The open end of the tube is then plugged with paper. When fired the pyrofuse burns through the line and operates the effect.

Solenoids
Electrically-energised solenoids are useful devices for remote control, but they consume a great deal of current and have only a short operating travel. For most efficient use they should be incorporated in mechanisms where they release levers, these taking the weight or the strain. A typical example is shown for a dropping box.

Trick line
If manual control is required three rings and a bar can support quite heavy loads. A quick snatch on the line tied to the bar releases the middle ring and drops whatever is attached to it.

Bowden cable
A stranded steel cable in a spring wound sheath (the normal choke or accelerator cable for cars) can be used for pulling or pushing remote items; it can also provide rotation. A simple application would be the turning of the hands of a clock situated in an inaccessible place in a studio.

Air balloon
A plastic tube with a balloon fixed at either end can act as a remote control device for certain purposes. Before being fitted one of the balloons is inflated to its full capacity so that when released the air pressure equalises, half inflating both balloons. When one balloon is squeezed the other expands. Useful for breathing dummies and pulsating nasties.

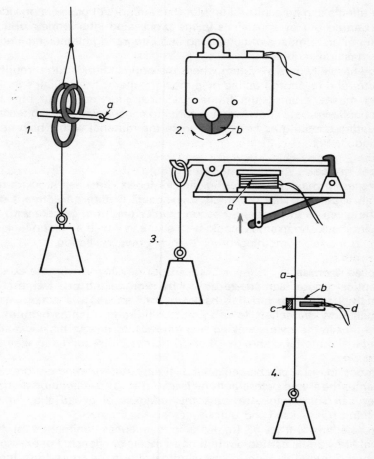

REMOTE CONTROL

Remote control devices must be simple and foolproof.
1. Three metal rings used as a simple release. A quick snatch on pull line (a) releases the weight. 2. Bomb release type with sideways-opening jaws (b) 3. Release using lever attached to solenoid (a) to hold heavy weight. 4. A nylon line passing between two holes in a metal tube is severed when a pyrofuse is ignited close to it. a, Nylon line. b, Metal tube. c, Plug. d, Pyrofuse.

Optical Printing

Many effects can be achieved on film that are not yet possible on video tape. Carried out by specialists in the processing laboratories, optical printing offers a means of combining and integrating filmed sequences in any fashion required.

Very basically, it is a system where the original film is run through a projector and re-photographed by a movie camera. The facilities for inserting masks, altering the frame size, changing the colour etc. are almost unlimited. It is however, essential to consult with the lab technician before shooting as he can only use the material with which he is supplied.

Optical mattes

An obscuring mask positioned in the printer as the fresh stock is run through allows an area to remain unexposed. Different treatment can then be given to this area in a second run through the camera with an opposite mask. An example could be a scene in which a person looking at a mirror sees something other than his own reflection.

Selected frames

The optical printer can freeze action by reproducing one frame continuously. It can also run film backwards to reverse the action.

It can slow the action down by stretch printing, such as by printing every other frame twice, making two frames into three. This is useful if the original material is shot at 16 or 18 frames per second and seems a bit jerky.

'Smoothing-out' can be achieved by lightly over-printing on the middle frame, the frame before and the frame after. These additional ghost images can sometimes eradicate the jerkiness of a bad shot where something has passed too quickly across the frame.

By selecting particular frames and sequences, animation of the original film can be carried out in time to music or speech. For example, trees and flowers blowing in the wind can be made to perform to an orchestral score or animals can have their mouth movements synchronised with words.

Comic animation

For some comic sequences it is not merely sufficient to alter the speed of the action. Where the movement is to appear unreal the optical printer can be programmed to select say, every fourth frame and print it four times, imparting a jerky mechanical movement to otherwise smooth action.

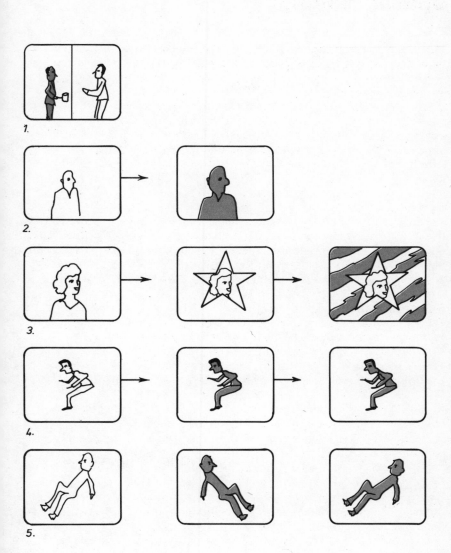

OPTICAL PRINTING

Many special effects can be achieved on film by the use of an optical printer which can modify both the subject material and the action. 1. Split screen effects. 2. Frame content can be enlarged. 3. Frame can have mask added and second background. 4. Frame can have action frozen. 5. Frames can be printed to give specific animation.

Further Reading

RAYMOND FIELDING:
The Technique Of Special Effects Cinematography. Focal Press/Hastings House.
An outstanding work on special techniques in motion-picture making. Orientated towards 'in-camera' and optical methods.

BERNARD WILKIE:
The Technique of Special Effects in Television. Focal Press/Hastings House. Covers a wide range of TV and motion picture effects.

FRANK. P. CLARK:
Special Effects in Motion Pictures. Society of Motion Pictures & TV Engineers Inc. New York.
The mechanics of motion picture effects. A practical and basic approach.

GERALD MILLERSON:
The Techniques of Television Production. Focal Press/Hastings House.
A comprehensive work covering most aspects of TV Production including scenic and lighting effects.

GERALD MILLERSON:
Basic TV Staging. Media Manual. Focal Press/Hastings House.
A concise handbook for those concerned with the design of TV shows.

THE REV. RONALD LANCASTER:
Fireworks, Principles and Practice. Chemical Publishing Co. Inc. New York.
Chemical formulae and manufacturing details expertly explained.

VICTOR H. WAGER:
Plaster casting. Alec Tiranti. London.
Detailed explanations of the processes used in mould making.

H. M. PERCY:
New Materials in Sculpture. Alec Tiranti, London.
Methods used in the casting of resins and the making of silicon rubber moulds.

Glossary

Acrylic Plastic (64, 82) The transparent, rigid plastic known as Perspex or Plexiglas

Beam Splitter (16) A semi-transparent sheet of optical glass that diverts some of the light that would normally pass through it.

Bomb Release (122) A solenoid-operated hook for releasing heavy weights or cables under tension.

Breakaway Glass (118) Plastic material used to imitate window glass where it has to be smashed. Made by pouring heated plastic onto metal sheets.

Bullet Hit (98) Plastic-cased detonator used to simulate a bullet striking its target. Electrically fired.

Case Mould (44) A flexible mould in two or more pieces backed with a rigid case to prevent it deforming.

Cel (22) Transparent plastic film on which is painted the pictures used in filmed animations.

Charcoal Tablet (72) Small circular tablets of compressed charcoal used for the burning of incense or for fuelling portable cooking stoves. Often impregnated with chemicals to facilitate lighting.

Chroma key (18) An electronic method of combining parts of television pictures received from separate cameras or other sources. Used chiefly for putting backgrounds behind action. Also known as colour separation overlay.

Cobweb Gun (134) Hand-held dispenser of latex 'cobweb' filaments.

Colour Separation Overlay (18) See Chroma Key.

Crab (50) Term used to describe camera movement when the dolly or pedestal is moved sideways.

Deflagration (84) The explosive effect of burning gunpowder.

Detonation (84) The shock effect which causes the explosion of high-explosive materials

Dolly A Wheeled truck on which cameras are mounted. Has steering and a moving arm which raises and lowers camera.

Dry Ice (60) Frozen carbon-dioxide gas in solid form. Used commercially for cold storage. When mixed with hot-water generates large quantities of water vapour in form of heavy mist

Dry Ice Generator (60) A box or vessel designed to liberate dry ice mist under controlled conditions.

Expanded Polystyrene (36) Attenuated, lightweight, rigid-foam, plastic material principally used for thermal insulation. Has many uses in the making of film and TV props.

Fade (32) Term used to describe the effect where picture fades into black. Cross-fade implies that as one picture fades down another 'fades' up to take its place.

Fifty-Fifty Mirror (28, 32) A mirror which has been only partially silvered or aluminised on one surface. Used for beam-splitting or superimposition effects.

Film Loop (130, 132) Term derived from the days when an endless loop of film was run through a back-projection machine or telecine equipment to provide a continuously running effect. Frequently used for rain, snow, fog and blizzard effects, but now as a conventional reel of film.

Flame Ark (78) Pitched-roof-shaped wire-netting frame on which impregnated cloth is burnt to provide high flames.

Flame Drum (12, 74) Motorised, transparent-plastic cylinder on which can be painted designs to throw shadows. Particularly useful for the simulation of leaping flames.

Flame Fork (74, 76) Trident-shaped pipe for the burning of gas during fire sequences in the studio.

Flash Pot (88) Cardboard carton containing pyrotechnic flashpowder for 'wizard' appearances and other flash effects in the studio. Usually electrically fired.

Flat Pack (88) A folded paper packet to contain pyrotechnic materials and a fuse. Used chiefly for small local effects.

Front-Axial Projection (16) (also called AXIAL-FRONT PROJECTION) A system of projecting photographs from a point near the camera to give large background scenes in the studio.

Glass Fibre (48) Fine filaments of drawn glass having very high tensile strength. Used in conjunction with polyester resin to produce the material commonly called fibreglass. Used in this form to make lightweight scenery and property items.

Glass Shot (14) A sheet of glass positioned between the camera and the scene can have part of the scene painted on it to extend the picture.

Inlay (14) Electronic method of combining part of one television picture with another. As the system requires the use of a cut out mask to define the area inlaid, the subject material must have finite edges.

Kaleidoscope (34) An arrangement of mirrors giving multiple images of a picture or a scene situated at their centre.

Lay-Up (48) Term used to describe the laminating of glass fibre and polyester resin.

Maroon (88, 96) A large explosive firework used to simulate the effects of shellfire. Also called a Ground Maroon.

Miniature (50) A model erected in front of the camera to appear as if part of the actual scene.

Mortar (88) A steel or heavy cardboard tube used to fire objects into the air.

Overlay (14) An electronic method of combining part of one television picture with another. Able to handle moving subjects in infinite arrangements. Uses black and white as triggering factors instead of the colour separation principle associated with colour separation overlay or chroma key.

Pan (34, 50) Term used to describe camera movement where it is swung to either side.

Pedestal Wheeled mounting for TV camera. Camera raised. and lowered on a central column.

Periscope (34) An arrangement of two mirrors which allows a higher or lower viewpoint to be obtained. Shots very close to the studio floor can be taken by a camera fitted with a periscope.

Piece Mould (44) A mould constructed in two or more pieces to facilitate the removal of the cast.

Polyester Resin (48) Resinous compound that when mixed with reagents hardens and solidifies. Used both for casting purposes and for the bonding of glass fibre lay-ups.

Pyrofuse (98) A small electrical fuse designed for the ignition of pyrotechnic materials.

Pyrotechnics (96) Fireworks, rockets, flares, thunderflashes etc., containing powdered materials which burn or explode when ignited.

Reflex Screen (16) Glass-beaded material supplied in the form of sheets or rolls can be applied to a backing or to a studio wall to form a projection screen. Known as a reflex screen it reflects almost all the light that hits it back to the point from which it came. This characteristic is the basis of the front-axial projection system.

Release Agent (40, 48) Substance applied to the surface of moulds to prevent adhesion of the casting compounds.

Rostrum (Animated Screen) Camera (22) A fixed movie camera mounted vertically above a work table. The camera, able to record one frame at a time, is used for film animation purposes.

Scenic Projection (16) The system of projecting large photographic images onto screens placed at the rear of the scene. A convenient method of providing realistic backings.

Smoke Gun (70) (or **Smoke Machine**) Portable machine to be carried in the hand or placed on the studio floor for the purpose of furnishing controlled amounts of smoke. Smoke is generated by the heating of oil.

Smoke Pot (72) Pyrotechnic smoke maker.

Solenoid (148) An electromagnetic device which imparts a limited movement to a steel core or armature.

Stop Motion (24) Term erroneously applied to the principle of single-frame film animation.

Telecine Machine (18) Equipment used to transmit movie film in the form of television pictures.

Thermoplastic (38) A material which softens when heated.

Tilt (50) Term used to describe camera movement when it is tipped up or down.

Track (34, 50) Term used to describe camera movement when the dolly or pedestal is moved towards or away from the scene.

Trick Line (148) A line which when pulled releases a catch or drops something.

Vacuum Forming (38) The method of sucking a heated sheet of plastic over a master item to reproduce its shape.

Whoofer (90) A compressed-air cylinder used to discharge pieces of material and dust into the air to resemble an explosion.

Wipe (32) A term used to describe the effect where one picture is removed by a line travelling across it to reveal a second picture.